Delights from Maharashtra

About Jaico Publishing House

Founded fifty-seven years ago, Jaico Publishing House has published over 1,600 titles in a diverse range of subjects such as adult and children's literature, history, humor, games, religion, philosophy, health, psychology and self-improvement. Our eminent authors include Sri Sri Paramahansa Yogananda (Autobiography of a Yogi), Khushwant Singh, Mulk Raj Anand, Kamala Markandaya, Eknath Easwaran, Nirad Chaudhuri, M.V. Kamath, Sarvapalli Radhakrishnan, Frank Morris, G.D. Khosla and Osho (Rajneesh).

Over the past two decades, Jaico has expanded its horizons to become a leading publisher of educational and professional books in business management, engineering and technology. Our college-level textbooks and reference titles are used by students countrywide. The success of our academic and professional titles is largely due to the efforts of our Educational and Corporate Sales Divisions.

Mr. Jaman Shah, our late founder, established Jaico in 1946 as a book distribution company. Sensing that independence was around the corner, he aptly named his company Jaico ("Jai" means victory in Hindi). In order to tap the significant demand for affordable books in a developing nation, Mr. Shah initiated Jaico's own publications. Jaico was India's first publisher of paperback books in the English language.

In addition to publishing its own titles, Jaico is a major distributor for its own books as well as those of leading global publishers such as McGraw Hill, Pearson, International Thomson and Elsevier Science. With its headquarters in Mumbai, Jaico has other sales offices in Delhi, Kolkata, Bangalore, Chennai, Hyderabad, and Ahmedabad. Our sales team of over forty executives, direct mail order division, and website ensure that our books effectively reach all urban and rural parts of the country.

DELIGHTS FROM MAHARASHTRA

By

Aroona Reejhsinghani

JAICO PUBLISHING HOUSE
Mumbai ● Delhi ● Bangalore ● Kolkata
Hyderabad ● Chennai ● Ahmedabad

© by Aroona Reejhsinghani

No part of this book may be reproduced or utilized in any form or by any means, electronic or mechanical including photocopying, recording or by any information storage and retrieval system, without permission in writing from the publishers.

DELIGHTS FROM MAHARASHTRA
ISBN 81-7992-518-1

First Jaico Impression: 1975
Second Jaico Impression: 1981
Third Jaico Impression: 1987
Fourth Jaico Impression: 1990
Fifth Jaico Impression: 1991
Sixth Jaico Impression: 1996
Seventh Jaico Impression: 1999
Eighth Jaico Impression: 2003

Published by:
Jaico Publishing House
121, Mahatma Gandhi Road
Mumbai - 400 001.

Printed by:
Sanman & Co.
113, Shivshakti Ind. Estate,
Marol Naka, Andheri (E),
Mumbai - 400 059.

CONTENTS

	Pages
Introduction	1
Glossary	3
Helpful hints	5
Lets go marketing	7
Cookery glossary	18

Vegetarian dishes

Bhopla cha bhurta	23
Bhopla cha panchamrut	23
Bhopla cha raita	23
Masalyachi vangi	24
Vangi ani batatechi bhaji	24
Stuffed brinjals	25
Vangicha bhurta	26
Kapachi vangi	26
Vangi cha ravaiya	26
Vangi cha raita	27
Brinjal curry	27
Kareli cha panchamrut	28
Stuffed bittergourds	29
Kareli cha khamam	29
Kareli chi bhajee	30
Kareli chi koshumbiri	30
Gajjar chi koshumbiri	31
Khaman kakadi	31
Kakadi cha raita	31
Arvi chi bhajee	32
Arvi curry	32

CONTENTS

	Pages
Corn curry	33
Corn and vegetable bhajee	33
Mirchi chi bhajee	34
Mirchi cha raita	35
Masalyachi mirchi	35
Capsicum in curds	36
Stuffed capsicums	36
Bund gobi chi koshumbiri	37
Bund gobi cha raita	37
Cauliflower bhajee	38
Dry chillies	38
Drumstick curry	39
Sweet and sour drumsticks	39
Drumstick pitla	40
Drumstick raita	41
Stuffed ladies fingers	41
Bhendi channa	42
Chutney potatoes	42
Batatechi bhajee	43
Peanut potatoes	43
Batatechi sukhi bhajee	44
Potato curry	45
Potato kheema	45
Tomato curry	46
Tamati cha sar	46
Tomato pitla	47
Tamatichi bhajee	47
Sweet and sour suran	48
Suran koshumbiri	49
Suran curry	49
Mango curry	50
Mango treat	50
Parval and val dalimbi	51

CONTENTS

Pages

Parvalchi bhajee	51
Jackfruit treat	52
Kela chi bhajee	52
Moongfali chi ghanti	53
Peanut curry	53
Buttermilk curry	54
Cocum curry	54
Vada curry	55
Coconut curry	56
Sago khichdi	56
Plain pitla	57
Panchamrut No. 1	57
Panchamrut No. 2	58
Poha bhajee	58
Batata poha	59
Khaman poha	60
Pohebhat	60
Koal poha	61

Pickles and chutneys

Hot mango pickle	65
Guramba	65
Sweet and sour mango pickle	65
Mango murraba	66
Hot lime pickle	66
Amla murraba	67
Amla pickle	67
Carrot pickle	68
Carrot murraba	68
Chilli pickle	69
Prawn pickle	69
Bhopla skin chutney	70

CONTENTS

Pages

Chutney of curry leaves 70
Lasun chi tikhat 70
Chilli chutney 70
Peanut chutney 71
Coconut chutney 71

Pulses and lentils

Masurchi amti 75
Katachi amti 75
Dal channa 76
Dal toovar 76
Whole moong 77
Spicy toovar dal 78
Varan 78
Dal moong 79
Sprouted beans 79
Usal 80
Sukhi chawli 80

Fish and eggs

Stuffed pomfret 85
Fish in masala 85
Fried pakoda pomfret 86
Spicy pomfret curry 86
Fish and potato curry 87
Special pomfret curry 88
Pomfret masaledar 88
Hot and spicy pomfret 89
Fried pomfret 89
Masaledar mackerel 90
Bombay duck kababs 90

CONTENTS

	Pages
Bangda curry	90
Prawn curry	91
Prawn fry	92
Prawn masala fry	92
Prawn bhajee sukha	93
Prawn and vegetable curry	93
Prawn and peas mix	94
Prawn and pumpkin curry	95
Fried prawns	95
Masalyachi anda	96
Eggs and potato curry	96
Especial egg curry	97

Mutton and Chicken

Mutton with cauliflower	101
Mutton with parval	101
Mutton bhopla	102
Mutton with potatoes	102
Mutton chaps masaledar	103
Spicy mutton	104
Mutton curry No. 1	104
Mutton curry No. 2	105
Mutton kofta curry	106
Poha kheema	107
Kheema brinjal mix	107
Kheema	108
Kheema-stuffed cauliflower	109
Kheema-stuffed bittergourds	109
Kheema-stuffed parval	111
Brain masaledar	111
Brain curry	111
Spicy liver	112

CONTENTS

Pages

Liver kababs	112
Chicken and peas curry	113
Chicken curry	113

Rice Recipes

Mutton pullao	117
Prawn pullao	117
Kheema pullao	118
Valchi khichdi	119
Kesari bhat	120
Mitha bhat	121
Tomato bhat	121
Mango bhat	122
Dal bhat	122
Masala bhat	123
Potato bhat	124

Tea-time Savouries

Batata vada	127
Kanda vada	127
Alu vadi	128
Chakali	128
Bhel puri	129
Coconut kabab	130

Sweets and Desserts

Dal ladu	133
Besan ladu	133
Rava & coconut ladu	134
Rava ladu	134

CONTENTS

	Pages
Til ladu	134
Boondi ladu	135
Shrikhandachi vadi	136
Tilchi vadi	137
Rus chi vadi	137
Tamatar chi vadi	137
Kaju chi vadi	138
Rava chi vadi	138
Narial chi vadi	139
Batate chi vadi	139
Parshad cha sheera	140
Narial che rus cha sheera	140
Ambache rus cha sheera	141
Batate cha sheera	141
Modakas	141
Cucumber cake	142
Dudhpak	143
Karanjia	143
Shrikhand	144
Rote	144
Anarasa	145
Bhareli keli	146
Basundi	146
Kaju poli	146
Khoya poli	147
Puran poli	147
Coconut poli	148
Sweet khaja	148
Basan karanjia	149
Suji karanjia	150
Petha karanjia	151
Sweet chakali	151
Dudhachi vadi	152

Cold drinks

Mango cooler	155
Ginger cooler	155
Jaggery cooler	155
Tamarind refresher	155
Cocum amrit	156
Mint Nector	156

Puries and Chapaties

Masala puri	159
Mithi puri	159
Sheera chapati	159
Tilgul chapati	160

INTRODUCTION

Facing the Arabian sea is the vast state of Maharashtra and out of this sea come many delicious and unusual seafoods. Sea food dishes are therefore in the foreground of Maharashtrian cuisine. There is a great demand for pomfret a fish with a deepsea flavour which forms a basis for many fine dishes. Besides sea foods, Maharashtrians are also very fond of coconut. Every morning, one finds the lady of the house busy grinding coconut and other spices on the grinding stone. Although it is a laborious task, the women do not mind it because without the addition of coconut and hot and spicy condiments no dish is said to be complete. Maharashtrians are also very fond of vegetables and some of their vegetarian recipes are really unique and interesting and very nutritious at the same time because most of them besides containing coconut also contain such protein giving foods like groundnuts, cashewnuts and sesame seeds. Although Maharashtrian cuisine has not gained national fame, it is really quite delicious and nutritionally well-balanced and once you develop a taste for it, you will want to try it again and again. Maharashtrians usually use peanut oil in everything, even for making pickles they use this oil, but you can use any other medium of cooking you like and the food will taste equally good. I must thank Mrs. L. Randive, Mrs. N. Nivegi, Mrs.

Samant and Mrs. V. Chende for giving me some of their valuable recipes to include in this book. All the recipes given here are tried and tested and exclusively from the state of Maharashtra.

AROONA REEJHSINGHANI.

GLOSSARY

English	Hindi	Marathi
Ashgourd	Petha	Bhopla
Banana	Kela	Keli
Brinjal	Baigan	Vangi
Bittergourds	Karela	Kareli
Carrots	Gajur	Gajur
Cucumber	Kheera	Kakadi
Collocasia	Arwi	Alu
Collocasia leaves	Arwi ka patta	Alu cha pan
Corn	Makkai	Makka
Capsicum	Bada mirchi	Mirchi
Cabbage	Patta gobi	Kobi
Cauliflower	Phoolgobi	Flower
Chilli	Hari mirchi	Mirchi
Gooseberry	Amla	Awra
Jackfruit	Katahul	Fanus
Ladies finger	Bhendi	Bhindi
Mango (raw)	Kacha aamb	Keri
Mango (ripe)	Aamb	Amb
Potato	Alu	Batata
Onion	Pyaj	Kanda
Peas	Mutter	Vatana
Snake gourd	Parval	Parval
Tomato	Tamatar	Tomati
Radish	Muli	Mula
Sweet potato	Shakurkand	Ratale
Yam	Zamin kand	Suran

Herbs :—

Corriander leaves	Dhania	Kothimbiri
Curry leaves	Gandhela	Kadhi limb
Ginger (dry)	Saunt	Saunth
Ginger	Adhruk	Ale
Garlic	Lasoon	Lasun
Mint	Pudina	Pudeena

Spices:—

Asafoetida	Hing	Hing
Cumin seeds	Jeera	Jeera
Corriander seeds	Sukha dhania	Dhane
Corriander powder	Pissa hua dhania	Dhane chi pud
Chilli powder	Pissi hui lalmirchi	Mirchi chi pud
Cloves	Lavang	Laung
Cinnamon	Dalchini	Dalchi

DELIGHTS FROM MAHARASHTRA

Cardamom	Elachi	Velchi
Big cardamom	Bada or kala elachi	Mota velchi
Fenugreek seeds	Methi ka beej	Methi
Mace	Javintri	Javintri
Mustard seeds	Rai	Rai
Poppy seeds	Khus khus	Khus khus
Sesame seeds	Til	Til
Sugar	Shakur	Sakur
Salt	Nimuk	Meet
Saffron	Kesar	Keshar

Pulses :—

Bengal gram	Channe ki dal	Channe chi dal
Black gram	Urad ki dal	Urad chi dal
Green gram	Moong ki dal	Moonga chi dal
Red gram	Masur ki dal	Masur chi dal
Tur gram	Toovar ki dal	Turi chi dal

Flours :—

Wheat flour	Gheun ka atta	Ghawa cha peet
Refined flour	Maida	Maida
Gram flour	Besan	Besan
Semolina	Suji	Rava

Dry fruits :—

Almonds	Badam	Badam
Cashewnuts	Kaju	Kaju
Coconut	Narial	Naral
Coconut (dry)	Copra	Copra
Dates	Khajur	Khajur
Dates (dry)	Kharik	Kharik
Pistachio nuts	Pista	Pista
Groundnuts	Moongfali	Buimoong
Raisins	Kishmish	Manaka or baidana

Miscellaneous :—

Basil	Cocum	Cocum
Beaten rice	Cheura	Poha
Jaggery	Gur	Gur.
Tamarind	Imli	Chinch
Sago	Sabudana	Sabudana

Helpful Hints

1. Remove fishy smell from fish by rubbing on it a paste made of gram flour, salt and vinegar Set aside for half an hour, then wash nicely before putting in any called for recipe.

2. To remove bitterness from bittergourds, peel them nicely then wash them thoroughly in four to five changes of water and then soak them in salted buttermilk for 15 minutes. Wash once again in 4 to 5 changes of water before preparing them.

3. In frying whole chillies always prick them at a few places. In this way they will not jump out of the pan at you when they are being fried.

4. Always keep coconuts with fibrous end facing upwards to avoid rotting.

5. A teaspoon of salt added to chilli powder preserves it longer.

6. Before putting fish to fry, always heat some salt in the pan, wipe off the salt with a piece of paper and then fry the fish. In this way it will not stick to the pan.

7. You can get double the amount of juice from limes, if before taking out the juice you boil them till soft.

8. To preserve oil in tin for a long period keep immersed in it a small piece of jaggery.

9. To prevent oil from spluttering, put in it a tiny piece of tamarind coated with salt.

10. Do not throw away the water in which you boil your vegetables. This water is not only very nutritious but also adds taste to foods like rice and curries if used in them. Even drained-out water of rice or rice kanji can be put to good use if it is used as a base for your curries and soups.

Let's go 'marketing'

Much of the pleasure of home life depends upon good cooking. But serving good nourishing meals which stimulate the appetite and give a high degree of satisfaction through eye-appeal, flavour and texture largely depends upon the type of ingredients you use in your dishes. Buy the best and the freshest ingredients available in the market for preparing your food if you want to belong to that enviable category of women who are known in the circle of their friends and acquaintances as the women who prepare and serve "perfect meals". I am giving you a few hints below which will tell you how to buy the best things whenever you go 'marketing.'

Chicken

When selecting chicken make sure that its heavy and fleshy. This can be judged by touching its legs and breast. Chickens having smooth legs, short spurs and soft bones are young and tender. While the old ones have stiff and horny looking feet, long spurs and stiff beaks and bones.

Eggs

When buying eggs first ascertain whether the eggs are fresh or not. Freshness of eggs can be tested by placing them in salt water solution. A fresh egg being heavier then the salt solution sinks to the bottom while a stale one floats upon the surface. Another way of seeing if the egg is fresh is to hold the egg between your fingers against a bright light: if the top and bottom ends are clear, the egg is good, but if one of the ends has a cloudy and a coloured appearance, it is an indication that the egg is bad.

Fish

When buying any fish make sure that the fish is firm, moist and elastic. The eyes should be bright and full and not sunken. The gills should be reddish pink in colour and the scales should be bright coloured, glossy and adhering to the skin, with no slime or odour. When buying fish you should always go in for smaller ones, as the big ones are almost tough and old. To know the freshness of pomfrets, press the eyes, if red liquid comes out from them then its an indication that they are bad and stale, but if white liquid oozes out then they are fresh and worth buying.

Shellfish

Crabs:—should always have muscular action in the claws which may be detected by pressing the eyes with your fingers. If there is no muscular action then the crabs are stale.

Prawns:—should be firm and crisp to the touch. with no slime and odour.

Oysters:—should have firmly closed shells. If they are open then they are dead and unfit for eating.

Pork

Pork should be smooth and cool to the touch and the rind should be thin.

Bacon

Bacon should have a thin rind, the flesh should be clear red and it should firmly adhere to the bone.

Mutton

When buying mutton see that it is firm and elastic to the touch and should scarcely moisten your fingers. Bad meat is generally wet, sodden and flabby and its flesh looks like parchment. If the meat is greenish in colour or a bad odour emanates from it, then its an indication that decomposition has set in. Meat should not have a pale pink or purple colour. Pale pink colour is a sign of disease and purple colour is an indication that the animal had died of disease before being slaughtered. Good meat is always firm and juicy and bright red in colour with plenty of white and hard fat adhering to it.

Vegetables

Brinjals......should be fairly firm, heavy for size with purple, smooth and glossy skin. The tops should have a fresh appearance and should be dark green in colour. Wilted, flabby and very soft vegetable with cracks and worm injury should be avoided.

Bittergourds......should be bright green in colour. Uniform in size, well-shaped, firm, tender and young. The seeds should be less than half grown and embedded in white pith. Brown spots, shrivelled skin, worm injury, over-grown seeds and reddish pith should be avoided.

Beets......should be well-shaped and bright red in colour, smooth and clean. Tops of beets should have fresh, green and crisp leaves. Dark purple colour and soft spots indicate over-ripeness. Also avoid beets with rough surface, deep cuts, bruises and shrivelled skin.

Cabbage......should be hard, heavy with a glossy surface with as few open leaves as possible. Avoid yellow and light ones with soft or too many open leaves with worm eaten edges.

Carrots........should be well-shaped, clean, fresh, smooth, tender and bright in colour. Discard wilted ones, pale-coloured and the ones with worm injury.

Cauliflower......The white creamy solid heads are better than the granular ones. The jacket leaves and stems should be fresh and crisp. Spreading of heads indicates over-blooming. Avoid the cauliflowers with a discoloured smudge or speckled surface which indicates insect infection.

Capsicums......If you like less pungent ones always go for larger ones. They should be bright green in colour, firm, tender, fresh, clean, crisp, thick, glossy and smooth. Avoid flabby, crinkled and faded ones.

DELIGHTS FROM MAHARASHTRA

Drumsticks......should be dark green in colour, smooth, fairly plump, firm and fresh in appearance. The seeds should be less than half-grown. Over-grown seeds, shrivelled appearance and brown spots on the skin is an indication of over-maturity.

Cucumbers......The smaller ones are more tender than the larger ones and are excellent for using in salads and for pickling. Choose firm, well-shaped with bright green colour. Avoid dull, brown discoloured ones with withered and shrivelled skins.

French beans......should have long green pods, bright green colour, fresh, tender, crisp and clean appearance. The seeds should be less than half grown. Tough wilted, rusty or stringy beans should be avoided as they indicate maturity.

Greens and herbs of all types......Always insist upon fresh, crisp, tender, clean and bright coloured leaves and stalks and free from insect-infested edges. Greens with tough fibrous stems, muddy or having wilted yellowish leaves should be rejected.

Ladies fingers......should be bright green colour from stems to tips without any brownish discoloration or limpness. They should be tender, young, clean and brittle. Hard, shrivelled, worm injury and soft vegetable indicates decay.

Onions......the fresh tender ones with green stalks (green or spring) onions are good for immediate consumption. The pink ones are more pungent then the white ones. The tiny white onions are sweet and used for making pickles or in curries and vegetables. Onions should be dry, firm to the touch, clean and bright. Onions with soft spots, worm injury or with a seed stem and very strong flavour are of poor quality.

Peas......should be bright green in colour, tender, fresh, crisp with well-filled pods. Avoid dried or wet ones that are stale and contain worms.

Potatoes......should be clean, firm and free from blemishes with thin and smooth peel. They should not be soft, withered or wrinkled with hollow brown spots. Green spots beneath the skin cause bitter flavour therefore they should not be bought.

Pumpkin......should be smooth, heavy with dark brown or green rind. The seeds should be less then half grown and the inside flesh should be firm and sweet. Pumpkins with cuts and bruises should be avoided.

Tindli......should be tender, firm, smooth and fresh in appearance with immature inner seeds. Over-mature inner seeds, reddish pith and shrivelled appearance are indication of decay.

Ribbed gourd......firm, young, smooth, tender and fresh in appearance. Very soft or shrivelled vegetable with worm injury or brown and soft spots should not be bought.

Radishes......are of two types: long white and round red ones. Round radishes should be plump, round and firm with bright red colour. Avoid those that are too big, over-mature with yellow and decayed stems. White radishes should be well-formed, thick with tapering ends and fresh, clean, crisp and tender leaves on top. Wilted tops, tough, woody or strong flavoured root indicates over-ripeness.

Tomatoes......the slightly green ones can be ripened at room temperature. The bigger ones have more flesh and are good for salads while the smaller ones have more juice and are good for making soups and curries. Tomatoes should be bright red in colour, firm, well-formed and unblemished and free from cracks. Wrinkled, soft, watery or with insect holes and cuts at the top are unfit for eating.

Turnips......should be fresh, young, tender, firm, smooth with green tops. Strong-flavoured, large, coarse with wilted leaves and stems and soft roots should be avoided.

Sweetpotatoes......should be well-shaped, firm, fresh with smooth purple skins Wet, soft, shrivelled and discoloured vegetable should be rejected.

Fruits

Apples......should be brilliant red in colour, glossy, juicy, firm, crisp, fresh clean and well-shaped. Mature but not over-ripe with juicy fine-textured and fine-flavoured flesh.

Apricots......should be orange, yellow or golden coloured. They should be plump, fairly firm, juicy, fresh and well-shaped.

Bananas......should have green, yellow or red colour. They should be plump, well-formed fruit with smooth unbroken skin. Soft and mushy bananas indicate decay. Discoloured, unbroken skin need not indicate injury to its flesh and therefore can be eaten.

Berries of all types......should be bright, clean, plump, fresh and free from trash. Dull, soft, limp, watery and wrinkled berries should be avoided.

Cherries......should be bright red in colour, fresh, firm, round and juicy. Before buying examine at stem ends for bruises, worm injury and decay.

Coconuts......should be green in colour, heavy for size and must have water inside. Unsound coconuts have wet or mouldy eyes.

Chickoo......should be deep brown in colour. Firm, juicy, tender, fresh and smooth fruit should be bought only. Soft and mushy fruit or fruit with hard spots should not be bought.

Custard apples......should have dark green colour skin with black spots. The fruit should be well-shaped, juicy, fairly firm with white and sweet flesh. Very hard and soft and watery fruit with cracked outer skin and thin flesh and worm injury should not be bought.

DELIGHTS FROM MAHARASHTRA

Dates......should have golden brown skin and should be lustrous, glossy, smooth and firm. Soft and mushy fruit should not be bought.

Figs......should either have greenish yellow or purplish to almost black colour. The fruit should be fairly soft but not mushy, plump and big. Small fruits do not have much taste.

Guavas......should have dark green or deep yellow exterior and red or white interior. The fruit should be smooth, glossy, fresh, fairly firm and well-shaped. Soft and pulpy fruit with soft dark spots and hard over-grown seeds should not be purchased.

Grapes......should be black, green or red coloured. The fruit should be plump, firm, smooth with thin skin. The flesh should be firmly attached to the stem and the bunches should be compact. Soft, mushy and shrivelled fruit should be avoided.

Lemons (sweet)......yellow, greenish yellow or deep yellow. Should be firm, heavy for size, clean, fresh, well-shaped and plump. Greenish yellow colour indicates immature fruit with high acid content. Deep yellow fruits are usually thin-skinned, juicier and sweet. Shrivelled, hard-skinned or soft, spongy fruits are old or dried out.

Mangoes......should have green, yellow, orange or red skin. Should be fresh, plump, firm having smooth and glossy skin and spicy aroma. Soft, spongy or shrivelled fruit should not be bought.

Musk melon......should have firm and smooth outer skin. The colour of the skin usually varies from whitish green and green rind to pale golden colour. Whitish green or green rind indicates immaturity. While golden colour indicates ripe fruit. It has juicy, sweet fine-flavoured and pink flesh. Ripeness in most kinds of melons is indicated by the softening of the fruit around the slight depressions at the blossom ends which yield to the pressure of the fingers. Usually the characteristic odour of melon becomes more pronounced when the full stage of ripeness has been reached.

Oranges......should have golden yellow peels Should be firm and heavy for size, smooth, well-shaped, juicy and fresh in appearance. Avoid soft, spongy and shrivelled fruits. A small spot of decay ruins the taste of the whole fruit. Surface blemishes such as scratches slight discolouration or greenish or brown areas do not affect the inner fruit. Smaller oranges have more juice and are more economical then larger ones.

Papaya......green or golden colour. Should be heavy for size, firm and fresh in appearance with a nice aroma. Dark green and hard fruit is unripe, whereas fruit with soft, brown spots indicates decay.

Pomogranates......Deep red or reddish brown rind. Should be well-shaped, heavy for size with smooth, glossy, thin and tough skins. There should be abundance of bright red juicy seeds enveloped in white or light pink pithy structure

DELIGHTS FROM MAHARASHTRA

Light pink outer skin, shrivelled, dried and hard fruit with light pink or white seeds should be avoided. Look for signs of decay in the pith and in the seeds.

Plums and prunes......should be plump, clean, smooth, fairly firm, free from scars and other skin defects. Softened tip indicates decay. Shrivelled and wrinkled fruit should not be bought.

Pineapple......golden orange colour. Should be fresh, clean and heavy fruit with flat eyes and rich fragrance. Spikes pull out easily if the fruit is ripe. Look for signs of decay at its bottom. Do not buy fruit with soft spots.

Pears......should be well-shaped, fresh and firm with smooth unbroken skin. When flesh yields gently to firm pressure at stem end it indicates ripeness. Wilted, shrivelled and soft fruit should not be purchased.

Peaches......should have golden yellow skin. Should be fresh, well shaped, firm, juicy, tender with unbroken skin. Pale, shrivelled and rubbery fruit should be avoided. Green fruit is sour and not ripe.

Watermelon......dark green rind. Should be glossy, fresh, well-shaped, firm and heavy for its size. Inner flesh should be crisp, juicy, sweet red and free from fibres. Soft and watery flesh indicates over-ripeness. Avoid decay at stem end. Test for ripeness by pluging.

COOKERY GLOSSARY

Beat......to beat with a rotary beater, fork or a spoon any liquid or semi-liquid food with the express purpose of mixing that food thoroughly and making it smooth.

Blend......to combine several ingredients together until smooth.

Boil......to heat a mixture or a liquid until bubbles appear on the surface and vapour starts rising.

Batter......is a mixture of flour and liquid. The consistency of batter is such that it can be stirred with a spoon, and is thin enough to pour or drop from a spoon.

Chill......to cool food by placing it over ice or in the fridge.

Chop......to cut food into small pieces.

Combine......to join two or more ingredients together.

Dice......to cut food into small pieces.

Dissolve......to melt.

Drain......to free a food completely from liquid.

Deep fry......to fry in plenty of boiling ghee or oil.

Dough......a mixture of flour and liquid usually with other ingredients added. A dough is thick enough to knead or to roll but is too stiff to stir or pour.

Flake......to separate food gently with a fork.

Fry......to cook food in boiling oil till golden.

Garnish......to decorate food.

DELIGHTS FROM MAHARASHTRA

Grate......to rub food into small pieces on a grater.

Grind......to reduce food to a paste.

Gravy......liquid in which the food is cooked.

Knead......to work dough with hands pressing, stretching and folding until it reaches a desired consistency.

Melt......to heat until the ingredients are changed from solid to liquid.

Mince......to chop food as finely as possible.

Mix......to stir different ingredients together.

Peel or blanch......to remove the outside skin or peel of vegetables or fruits.

Puree......a very smooth sauce obtained from vegetables or fruits by rubbing them through a sieve.

Roll......to place a small ball of dough on a flat wooden board and roll it out into any shape you like with the help of a rolling pin.

Sift......to separate coarse pieces from flour, sugar ecetera by shaking through a sieve.

Seasonings......aromatic dried herbs used to increase the taste and appearance of food.

Shred......to cut foods into small, long and narrow pieces.

Squeeze......to drain out the liquid from the food by crushing or pressing it between your hands.

Simmer......to cook food just below the boiling point.

Soak......to cover the food with liquid.

Shallow fry......to fry food in little boiling ghee till brown.

Stalk......an individual piece in corriander or mint. For example the various stalks of mint make a bunch of mint. In the same way a garlic flake is a part of a pod of garlic. A number of flakes of garlic make up a pod of garlic.

VEGETARIAN DISHES

Bhopla cha bhurta

250 grams red bhopla, peeled and grated. 3 tblsps. finely grated coconut. 1 tsp. mustard seeds. Handful of corriander leaves. $\frac{1}{4}$ tsp. turmeric powder. Salt and chilli powder to taste.

Heat 2 tblsps. oil and toss in the mustard seeds, when they stop popping, add all the spices, mix well, then add bhopla, coconut and salt. Cover tightly and cook without adding water till the bhopla is tender. Serve garnished with corriander leaves.

Bhopla cha panchamrut

1 kilo red bhopla. $\frac{1}{4}$ dry coconut. 1 tblsp. each of til and khuskhus. $\frac{1}{2}$ tsp. mustard seeds. A pinch of asafoetida. Handful of corriander leaves. $\frac{1}{2}$ tsp. turmeric powder. 4 green chillies, minced. 1 lime-sized ball of tamarind. 1 tblsp. grated jaggery. Salt and chilli powder to suit the taste.

Cover tamarind with 1 cup water for 5 minutes and then squeeze out its juice. Dissolve jaggery in tamarind water. Peel and cut bhopla into small pieces. Fry coconut, til and khuskhus to a red colour and grind to a paste. Heat 2 tblsps. oil and toss in asafoetida and mustard seeds, when the seeds stop popping, add turmeric, chillies and salt Cover tightly and cook without adding water over a slow fire till it is almost done. Put in the tamarind and coconut paste and continue cooking till the vegetable is done. Serve decorated with corriander leaves.

Bhopla cha raita

150 grams red bhopla, peeled and sliced. 100

grams thick curds, beaten nicely. 2 green chillies, minced. Handful of sliced corriander leaves. ¼ tsp. mustard seeds. 1 tsp. sugar. Pinch of asafoetida. Salt to suit the taste.

Put chillies and bhopla together in a vessel. Add salt and cook over a low fire without adding water till tender. Remove from fire and mash to a paste and then mix with curds. Also put in sugar and mix well. Heat 1 tblsp. oil and put in asafoetida and mustard. When the seeds stop popping, pour over the raita. Serve sprinkled with corriander leaves.

Masalyachi vangi

2 medium brinjals, sliced. ¼ coconut. 1 small onion. 1 tblsp. corriander seeds. A few peppercorns. 4 cloves. 2 medium onions, minced. ½ tsp. turmeric powder. Handful of corriander leaves. Salt to taste.

Fry coconut, small onion, corriander seeds, peppercorns and cloves to a red colour and grind to a paste. Heat 2 tblsps. oil and fry minced onions to almond colour. Add brinjals, salt and turmeric. Cover tightly and cook without adding water over a slow fire till done. Mix in the coconut paste and remove from fire. Serve decorated with corriander leaves.

Vangi ani batatechi bhajee

2 medium brinjals, sliced. 2 medium potatoes, peeled and sliced. A pinch of asafoetida. 1 medium onion, minced. 1 tsp. mustard seeds. ½ tsp. turmeric powder. A few peppercorns. 1-inch

piece cinnamon. 3 green chillies. 1-inch piece ginger. $\frac{1}{4}$ coconut. 1 big tomato, peeled and sliced. Handful of corriander leaves. Salt to taste.

Grind peppercorns, cinnamon, chillies, ginger and coconut to a paste. Heat 2 tblsps. oil and toss in mustard seeds and asafoetida. When the seeds stop spluttering, put in the onion and fry till soft. Add all the spices, brinjals and potatoes. Mix well, put in the tomato. Cover tightly and cook without adding water till the vegetables are almost done. Add the coconut paste and continue cooking till the vegetables are tender. Serve decorated with corriander leaves.

Stuffed brinjals

250 grams small brinjals. 1 big onion. 4 green chillies. Handful of corriander leaves. $\frac{1}{2}$ tsp. turmeric powder. 1 tsp. grated jaggery. 1 tsp. mustard seeds. Pinch of asafoetida. $\frac{1}{4}$ dry coconut. 1-inch piece cinnamon stick. 4 cloves. A few peppercorns. A few pods tamarind. Salt to suit the taste.

Wash the brinjals and cut into four halfway through. Fry copra, cinnamon, cloves and peppercorns to a red colour and grind to a paste along with onion, chillies, corriander leaves, jaggery and tamarind. Mix in salt and turmeric and stuff into the brinjals. Heat 4 tblsps. oil and toss in the asafoetida and mustard seeds. When the seeds stop popping, put in the brinjals. Cover tightly and cook without adding water over a slow fire till the brinjals are done. Serve hot.

Vangicha bhurta

1 big brinjal. 1 medium onion, minced. Handful of sliced corriander leaves. 2 green chillies, minced. 4 tblsps. grated coconut. ½ tsp. each of pepper and chilli powder. Salt to taste.

Hold brinjal over open or gas flame till the skin turns black and wrinkled. Toss in cold water, peel and mash to a paste. Heat 2 tblsps. oil and fry onion and chillies till soft. Add salt, brinjals, coconut and spices and mix thoroughly. Serve decorated with corriander leaves.

Kapachi vangi

1 large and round brinjal. 4 tblsps. gram flour. ½ tsp. sugar. 1 tblsp. corriander powder. 1 tsp. ground cumin seeds. ½ tsp. turmeric powder. Salt to taste.

Cut the brinjal into 1-inch thick round pieces. Mix together all the remaining ingredients. Apply a little oil to all the pieces and pierce holes in them nicely and thoroughly with a fork. Fill with gram flour mixture. Heat 4 tblsps. oil and put in the pieces. Cover tightly and cook without adding water over a slow fire till crisp turning them occasionally. Serve hot.

Vangi cha ravaiya

250 grams brinjals. 25 grams til or sesame seeds. ½ tsp. garam masala 1 tblsp. corriander powder. ½ coconut, grated. Handful corriander leaves. 2 green chillies, minced. 1 tblsp. grated jaggery. ½ tsp. turmeric powder. Salt to suit the taste.

Roast and pound the til. Grind coconut, corriander leaves, chillies and jaggery to a paste. Heat 2 tblsps. oil and put in the brinjals and fry lightly. Add ground paste and til, mix well and put in 1 cup water. Cover and cook till the brinjals are tender and gravy thick. Serve decorated with corriander leaves.

Vangi cha raita

1 big brinjal. 100 grams thick curds, beaten nicely. 2 green chillies minced. ½ tsp. sugar ½ tsp. cumin seeds. Pinch of asafoetida. Handful corriander leaves. 1 tblsp. grated coconut. Salt to taste.

Roast the brinjal over open flame or gas fire till the skin turns black and wrinkled. Toss in cold water, peel and mash to a paste. Mix together brinjals, curds, salt, sugar and chillies. Heat 1 tblsp. oil and toss in asafoetida and cumin seeds. When the seeds stop popping, put into the curds. Serve decorated with corriander leaves and coconut.

Brinjal curry

500 grams small brinjals. 1 tblsp. cumin seeds. 1 tsp. turmeric powder. 1 tsp. peppercorns. 1-inch piece ginger. 3 large flakes garlic. 10 green chillies. ¼ tsp. garam masala. 1 lime-sized ball of tamarind. 2 tblsps. grated jaggery. Handful corriander leaves. 2 medium tomatoes, peeled and sliced. Salt to taste.

Grind green chillies, cumin seeds, ginger and garlic to a smooth paste. Cover tamarind with half cup water for 5 minutes, then squeeze out the Juice. Stir in jaggery and set aside. Heat 4 tblsps. oil and toss in a few curry leaves, then add brinjals, salt, ground paste and all the spices and tomatoes. Cover tightly and cook without adding water till the brinjals are almost done. Put in the tamarind water and continue cooking till the brinjals are tender. Serve decorated with corriander leaves.

Kareli cha panchamrut

250 grams bittergourds. 25 grams til or sesame seeds. 25 grams raisins. 50 grams roasted groundnuts. 10 cashewnuts. $\frac{1}{4}$ coconut, finely sliced. 25 grams grated jaggery. A few pods tamarind. A few peppercorns. 1 tsp. garam masala. 3 red chillies, broken. $\frac{1}{2}$ tsp. mustard seeds. Salt to taste.

Roast til and pound to a coarse powder with groundnuts and cashewnuts. Powder peppercorns. Cover tamarind with water for 5 minutes, then squeeze out the pulp. Peel bittergourds and remove bitterness......see Helpful Hints. Cut into small pieces. Heat 4 tblsps. oil and fry the bittergourds to a pale golden colour. Put in the rest of the above ingredients with the exception of red chillies and mustard seeds. Cover tightly and cook till the vegetable is tender and gravy thick. Remove from fire and set aside. Heat 1 tblsp. oil and toss in the chillies and mustard. When the mixture turns red, put into the panchamrut. Serve hot.

Stuffed bittergourds

250 grams thick bittergourds of equal size. 4 tblsps. gram flour. 3 tsps. sugar. 1 tblsp. corriander powder. 1 tsp. ground cumin seeds. Salt and chilli powder to taste.

Remove bitterness from gourds......see Helpful Hints, then cut on one side halfway through. Fry gram flour in a little oil to a red colour and mix in the rest of the above ingredients. Stuff into the gourds and tie with a thread. Heat 5 tblsps. oil and put in the gourds. Cover tightly and cook without adding water over a slow fire till done. Serve hot.

Karelicha khamam

1 cup channa dal. 250 grams bittergourds. 1 tsp. mustard seeds. Pinch of asafoetida. 1 tblsp. corriander powder. $\frac{1}{2}$ tsp. turmeric powder. 1 tsp. ground cumin seeds. 1 tblsp. sugar. A few pods tamarind. Handful or corriander leaves. Salt to taste.

Peel and remove bitterness from gourds......see Helpful Hints. Cut into small pieces and set aside. Soak dal whole night in water. Next morning, drain out the water and grind coarsely. Heat 4 tblsps. oil and toss in asafoetida and mustard. When the seeds stop popping, add gourds and fry till pale golden colour. Put in the rest of the above ingredients with the exception of tamarind and corriander leaves. Cover tightly and cook without adding water till the vegetable is done. Now cover tamarind with water for 5 minutes and squeeze out its juice, put into the cooked vegetable, mix well and remove from fire. Serve decorated with corriander leaves.

Kareli chi bhajee

250 grams bittergourds. ¼ coconut. 1 big onion 4 cloves. 1-inch piece cinnamon stick. A few peppercorns. A pinch asafoetida. ½ tsp. mustard seeds. 1 lime-sized ball tamarind. 2 tblsps. grated jaggery. Salt and chilli powder to taste. Handful of corriander leaves.

Peel and remove bitterness from gourds......see Helpful Hints. Cut into small pieces. Fry coconut, onion, cloves, cinnamon and peppercorns to a red colour and grind to a paste. Cover tamarind with 1 cup water for 5 minutes and squeeze out the juice. Heat 3 tblsps. oil and toss in asafoetida and mustard. When the seeds stop popping, add gourds and fry lightly. Put in all the above ingredients with the exception of corriander leaves. Cook till the gourds are tender. Serve decorated with corriander leaves.

Kareli chi koshumbiri

2 medium bittergourds. 2 green chillies, minced. 1 medium onion, minced. ¼ grated coconut. 1 tsp. ground cumin seeds. Salt and chilli powder to taste.

Remove bitterness from gourds......see Helpful Hints. Cut into very thin rings and deep fry till crisp and golden. Drain thoroughly and mix in the rest of the above ingredients before serving.

Gajjar chi koshumbiri

150 grams carrots, peeled and grated. 100 grams thick curds. 25 grams roasted and pounded groundnuts. 2 green chillies, minced. 1 tsp. sugar. A pinch asafoetida. 1 tsp. cumin seeds. Handful of corriander leaves.

Mix curds with carrots, groundnuts, chillies, sugar and salt. Heat 1 tblsp. oil and toss in asafoetida and cumin seeds. When the seeds stop popping, put into the carrots. Serve decorated with corriander leaves.

Khaman kakadi

100 grams cucumbers, peeled and grated. 25 grams roasted and pounded groundnuts. 1 tblsp. grated coconut. $\frac{1}{2}$ tsp. sugar. $\frac{1}{2}$ tsp. cumin seeds. Pinch of asafoetida. Handful of corriander leaves. Salt and lime juice to taste.

Mix together cucumber, nuts, coconut, sugar, salt and lime juice. Heat 1 tblsp. oil and toss in hing and cumin seeds. When they stop popping, put into the cucumber. Serve decorated with corriander leaves.

Kakadi cha raita

100 grams cucumber, peeled and grated. 100 grams curds. Handful of sliced corriander leaves. $\frac{1}{2}$-inch piece ginger, minced. 1 small firm tomato, diced. 1 tblsp. grated coconut. $\frac{1}{4}$ tsp. mustard seeds. 1 tsp. sugar. Pinch of asafoetida. Salt to taste.

Mix together curds, cucumber, ginger, tomato, sugar and salt. Heat 1 tblsp. oil and put in mustard and asafoetida, when the seeds stop popping, put into the curds. Serve decorated with coconut and corriander leaves.

Arvi chi bhaji

500 grams arvi or collocasia, peeled and sliced. $\frac{1}{2}$ tsp. turmeric powder. 4 flakes garlic. 4 green chillies. Lime sized ball of tamarind. 1 tblsp. grated jaggery. 1 tsp. ground cumin seeds. Handful of corriander leaves. Salt and chilli powder to taste.

Grind chillies and garlic to a paste. Mix with salt and spices and apply on arvi. Cover tamarind with 1 cup water for 5 minutes and squeeze out the juice, mix in the jaggery. Heat 2 tblsps. oil and add arvi, fry briefly and then pour in tamarind water. Cover tightly and cook till the vegetable is done. Serve decorated with corriander leaves.

Arvi curry

1 bunch collocasia leaves, finely sliced. 25 grams each of cashewnuts and peanuts. 25 grams channa dal. 1 small piece dry coconut. 1 small ball tamarind. 1 tblsp. grated jaggery. 1 tblsp. corriander powder. 1 tsp. ground cumin seeds. $\frac{1}{2}$ tsp. turmeric powder. 1 tsp. gram flour. $\frac{1}{4}$ tsp. mustard seeds. A pinch asafoetida. Salt and chilli powder to taste.

Soak peanuts and dal in water for a few hours. Drain and peel the peanuts. Slice dry coconut finely and roast to a red colour. Cover tamarind with water for 5 minutes and squeeze out the pulp. Put in jaggery. Heat 2 tblsps. oil and toss in the asafoetida and mustard, when the seeds stop popping, put in the leaves, dal, coconut, peanuts, cashewnuts, salt and all the spices. Fry for few minutes, then pour in 3 cups water. Cover and cook till the dal and leaves are almost done, then put in the tamarind juice. Continue cooking till the vegetable is cooked. Blend the gram flour with a little water and add to the curry. Simmer till the curry turns a little thick. Serve hot.

Corn curry

3 cobs of corn, boiled and cut into 2-inch pieces. 250 grams tomatoes, blanched and sliced. 2 cups coconut milk. Handful corriander leaves. 1 small onion, minced. 3 green chillies. 3 red chillies. 1 tsp. each of cumin and corriander seeds. 6 peppercorns. $\frac{1}{2}$ tsp. turmeric powder. Salt to taste.

Grind chillies and all the spices to a paste. Heat 2 tblsps. oil and fry onion till soft. Add corns and ground paste and fry for 5 minutes. Put in the tomatoes and salt and cook till the tomatoes turn soft. Put in the coconut milk and continue cooking till the curry turns a little thick. Serve decorated with corriander leaves.

Corn and vegetable bhajee

6 tender corn cobs, cut into 1-inch pieces. $\frac{1}{4}$ bunch each of spinch and chowlai sag. Handful

of sliced corriander leaves. 5 green chillies. 1-inch piece ginger. 1 tblsp. grated coconut. 2 cups thin coconut milk. ½ kilo mixed vegetables like potatoes, peas, pumpkin, sweet potatoes, cucumber, banana, carrots, cauliflower and french beans. ½ tsp. turmeric powder. Salt to taste. ½ cup thick coconut milk.

Clean, peel and cut all the vegetables into small pieces. Chop the spinch and chowlai. Grind ginger, chillies and coconut. Take a large vessel and heat 4 tblsps. oil in it. Mix in the ground coconut paste and turmeric and 1 tblsp. ground cumin seeds, arrange all the cobs on the masala, spread half of the greens on this, and spread all the vegetables on the leaves and lastly spread on top the remaining greens. Pour in the thin coconut milk. Cover the vessel tightly and cook over a slow fire till the vegetables are cooked. Pour in the thick coconut milk and simmer for 5 more minutes. Serve garnished with corriander leaves.

Mirchi chi bhajee

250 grams capsicums, cut finely. 25 grams roasted and pounded peanuts. ½ tsp. mustard seeds. A pinch asafoetida. 1 tblsp. grated coconut. Handful corriander leaves. A few pods tamarind. 2 tblsps. sliced raisins. 1 tsp. garam masala. Salt to taste.

Cover tamarind with water for 5 minutes and squeeze out the pulp. Heat 2 tblsps. oil and toss in mustard and asafoetida. When the seeds stop popping, add the capsicums, fry briefly, put in salt and ½ tsp. turmeric powder and 1 cup water. Cover and cook till the capsicums are almost done, then add garam masala, peanuts, tamarind and raisins and continue cooking till the capsicums are done. Serve garnished with coconut and corriander leaves.

Mirchi cha raita

2 capsicums, washed and shredded. 100 grams thick and beaten curds. ½ tsp. garam masala. Handful of corriander leaves. 1 tsp. sugar. 1 tsp. cumin seeds. Salt and chilli powder to suit the taste.

Mix capsicums with curds along with salt, sugar and corriander leaves. Sprinkle on top garam masala and chilli powder. Heat 1 tblsp. ghee and toss in the cumin seeds. When they stop popping, put over the curds.

Masalayachi mirchi

250 grams capsicums, cut finely. 100 grams onions, finely sliced. Lime-sized ball of tamarind. 1 tblsp. grated jaggery. 1 tblsp. grated coconut. ½ tsp. each of turmeric powder and garam masala. Handful of corriander leaves. ½ tsp. mustard seeds. Pinch of asafoetida. Salt to taste.

Heat 3 tblsps. oil and put in asafoetida and mustard. When the seeds stop popping, add mirchi and onions and fry till little red. Put in tamarind after squeezing from it 1 cup juice, jaggery, salt and all the spices. Cover and cook till the capsicums are done and gravy quite thick.

Serve decorated with coconut and corriander leaves.

Capsicum in curds

250 grams capsicums, cut finely. 1 cup beaten curds. ½ tsp. turmeric powder. ½ tsp. each of cumin seeds and garam masala. Pinch of asafoetida. 1 small piece coconut. 2 green chillies. 1-inch piece ginger. Handful of corriander leaves. 1 tblsp. grated jaggery. Salt to taste.

Dilute the curds with half cup water. Heat 2 tblsps. oil and toss in asafoetida and cumin seeds. When the seeds stop popping, put in the ground coconut, chillies, ginger. Mix nicely, then add capsicums and fry till little red. Put in the curds and all the spices and salt. Cover and cook till the capsicums are almost done, put in the jaggery and continue cooking till the capsicums are done and gravy thick. Serve hot decorated with corriander leaves.

Stuffed Capsicums

6 medium capsicums. ½ cup gram flour. 1 tblsp. corriander powder. 1 tsp. each of garam masala and ground cumin seeds. 2 medium onions, minced. 2 green chillies, minced, Handful of corriander leaves. 1 small ball tamarind. 2 cups coconut milk. 1 small piece ginger, minced. Salt and chilli powder to taste.

Make a slit halfway through on one side of each mirchi and set aside. Fry gram flour in a little oil to a red colour. Also fry onion, ginger and

DELIGHTS FROM MAHARASHTRA

chillies to a pale golden colour, mix in gram flour and salt and all the spices and stuff into each capsicum. Heat 4 tblsps. oil and fry the capsicums gently till they change colour. Pour in the coconut milk and add tamarind after extracting half cup juice from it. Cover and cook till the capsicums are tender and gravy thick. Serve garnished with 1 tblsp. grated coconut and corriander leaves.

Bund gobi chi koshumbiri

1 medium cabbage, shreded. ½ cup whole moong dal. ½ coconut, finely grated. A pinch asafoetida. 1 tsp. ground cumin seeds. ½ tsp. mustard seeds. 3 green chillies, minced. Handful corriander leaves. Salt and chilli powder to taste. Juice of half lime.

Soak dal whole night in water. Next morning, drain out the water and set aside. Heat 1 tblsp. ghee, add mustard and asafoetida. When the seeds stop popping, put in the dal and stir for 2 minutes. Mix in the cabbage, coconut, chillies and ground cumin seeds. Remove from fire, mix in lime juice and decorate with chopped corriander.

Bund gobi cha ratia

2 tblsps. finely shreded cabbage. 1 cup beaten curds. A few roasted groundnuts. A few cashewnuts. 1 tblsp. raisins. 2 green chillies, minced. 1 tiny piece ginger, minced. Handful of sliced corriander leaves. ¼ tsp. garam masala. ½ tsp. cumin seeds. Salt to taste.

Chop cashewnuts and groundnuts and raisins. Mix together curds, cabbage, nuts, raisins, salt, ginger, chillies and garam masala. Heat 1 tblsp. oil and toss in cumin seeds, when they stop popping, put into the curds. Serve decorated with corriander leaves.

Cauliflower bhajee

1 head cauliflower, broken into flowerets. ¼ coconut, finely grated. 1 cup coconut milk. 2 cloves. ¼-inch piece cinnamon stick. 1 cardamom 2 flakes garlic. 1-inch piece ginger. 2 green chillies. Handful of corriander leaves. A pinch asafoetida. 1 tsp. mustard seeds. ½ tsp. turmeric powder. Salt and chilli powder to taste.

Roast coconut, whole spices with the exception of mustard, ginger and garlic and grind to a smooth paste. Heat 2 tblsps. oil and toss in asafoetida and mustard. When the seeds stop popping, put in 1 medium onion, minced and chillies and fry till soft. Add cauliflower salt and turmeric and fry it to a light red colour. Put in coconut paste and coconut milk. Cover tightly and cook over a slow fire till the cauliflower is tender and gravy thick. Serve decorated with corriander leaves.

Dry chillies

100 grams long and thick chillies. 1 cup beaten curds. Salt to taste.

Wash and make a slit halfway through in each chilli. Mix together salt and curds. Put the chillies in curds and set aside for 24 hours. Then place on a plastic sheet and dry in the sun. In the evening remove from the sun and put once again into the curds and in the next morning put again in the sun. Do this for 3 days then keep on placing the chillies in the sun regularly without putting into the curds till the chillies turn dry thoroughly. Store in airtight container. When wanted for use deep fry them quickly over a gentle fire to a light golden colour, otherwise they will get burnt.

Drumstick curry

4 drumsticks, scraped and cut into small pieces. $\frac{1}{2}$ Coconut, 1 medium onion 3 red chillies $\frac{1}{2}$ tsp. each of peppercorns and cumin seeds. 1 tsp. corriander seeds. 2 tblsps. tamarind juice. $\frac{1}{2}$ tsp. turmeric powder. $\frac{1}{2}$ tsp. mustard seeds. Pinch asafoetida. Handful of corriander leaves. Salt to taste.

Roast coconut, onion, chillies, peppercorns, corriander and cumin seeds and grind to a paste. Heat 2 tblsps. oil and toss in mustard and asafoetida. When the seeds stop popping, put in drumsticks, salt and turmeric. Mix well and fry for a few minutes. Pour in 2 cups water and cook till the drumsticks are almost done. Add coconut paste and tamarind and continue cooking till the vegetable is done. Serve decorated with corriander leaves.

Sweet and sour drumsticks

4 drumsticks, scraped and cut into small pieces.

1 small ball tamarind. 1 tblsp. grated jaggery. 1 medium onion, minced. 1½ tblsps. gram dal, boiled. ½-inch piece ginger. 4 flakes garlic. 1 small piece dry coconut. ½ tsp. cumin seeds. 1 tsp. corriander seeds. ½ tsp. turmeric powder. 2 green chillies. Handful of sliced corriander leaves. A pinch asafoetida. ½ tsp. garam masala. Salt and chilli powder to taste.

Half boil the drumsticks in salted water and drain. Cover tamarind with water for 5 minutes then squeeze out the juice. Roast coconut and grind to a paste along with ginger, garlic, chillies, corriander and cumin seeds. Heat 3 tblsps. oil and put in onions and asafoetida. Fry the onion to a golden colour. Sprinkle a little water and add ground coconut paste, salt and chilli powder and fry till the oil starts oozing out. Add dal, drumsticks and 1 cup water. Cook till the drumsticks are almost done, then put in tamarind and jaggery and continue cooking till they are tender. Serve decorated with corriander leaves.

Drumstick pitla

2 drumsticks. 1 cup gram flour. 1 small onion. 1 flake garlic. 2 green chillies. 1 small piece dry coconut. ¼ tsp. mustard seeds. Pinch of asafoetida. ½ tsp. garam masala. ½-inch piece ginger. Handful of sliced corriander leaves. A few pods tamarind. ½ tsp. turmeric powder. 1 tsp. ground cumin seeds. Salt and chilli powder to taste.

Cover tamarind with 1 cup water for 5 minutes, then squeeze out the juice. Roast and grind the coconut. Grind coarsely onion, ginger, garlic and chillies. Boil drumsticks till soft, remove inner soft pith of drumsticks and set aside. Heat 2 tblsps. oil and toss in mustard seeds and asafoetida, when the seeds stop popping, add gram flour and fry till a nice smell emanates from it. Put in 2 cups water along with all the above ingredients with the exception of corriander leaves and keep on stirring over a fire till the mixture turns thick and dry. Serve garnished with corriander leaves and accompanied by puries.

Drumstick raita

1 drumstick. 1 cup beaten curds. 2 green chillies, minced. Handful corriander leaves. 1 tiny piece minced ginger. ½ tsp. cumin seeds. 1 tsp. grated coconut. A few roasted peanuts, pounded coarsely. Salt to taste.

Boil drumstick and remove its pith. Mix all the above ingredients together with the exception of cumin seeds and corriander leaves. Heat 1 tsp. oil and toss in cumin seeds, when they stop popping, put into the curds. Serve decorated with chopped corriander.

Stuffed ladies fingers

250 grams big ladies fingers. 4 tblsps. gram flour. 1 small piece finely grated coconut. Handful of sliced corriander leaves. 2 green chillies. 2 flakes garlic. 1 medium onion. 1 small piece ginger. 1 tblsp. corriander powder. 1 tsp. ground cumin seeds. ½ tsp. turmeric powder. Salt and chilli powder to taste.

Make a slit in each bhendi halfway through Grind corriander, garlic coconut, ginger and chillies to a paste and mix with gram flour. Add salt and all the spices and stuff into bhendies. Heat 6 tblsps. oil and fry the vegetables till red and crisp. Drain and serve piping hot.

Bhendi channa

100 grams tender ladies fingers. 125 grams whole channa. $\frac{1}{2}$ tsp. turmeric powder. A few pods tamarind. 1 tblsp. grated coconut. 1 tsp. cumin seeds. 1 tsp. corriander seeds. 1-inch piece ginger 2 flakes garlic. Handful of corriander leaves. Salt and chilli powder to taste.

Soak channa whole night in water. Next morning, boil in the water in which they were soaked till soft. Cut bhendies into 1-inch pieces and fry to a pale gold colour. Cover tamarind with water for 5 minutes then squeeze out the juice. Grind coconut, garlic, ginger and 2 green chillies and all the spices to a paste. Heat 2 tblsps. oil and toss in a pinch of asafoetida and $\frac{1}{2}$ tsp. mustard seeds. When the seeds stop popping, add the ground paste and fry nicely, put in the channas, salt and turmeric and bhendi and mix well. Pour tamarind water on top. Cook till the gravy turns a little thick. Serve docorated with corriander leaves.

Chutney potatoes

4 medium potatoes. 1 bunch corriander leaves. 4 green chillies. 1-inch piece ginger. 4 flakes garlic. 1 small piece coconut. A few pods tamarind (op-

DELIGHTS FROM MAHARASHTRA

tional). 1 tsp. cumin seeds. 1 tsp. corriander seeds. ½ tsp. turmeric powder. ¼ tsp. each of cumin and mustard seeds. Salt and chilli powder to taste.

Peel and cut the potatoes into round slices. Grind corriander chillies, ginger, garlic, coconut, tamarind, tsp. of cumin seeds and corriander seeds to a very fine paste. Mix with salt, turmeric and chilli powder and apply nicely on the potato slices. Heat 3 tblsps. oil and toss in cumin and mustard seeds. When the seeds stop popping, put in the potato slices. Cover tightly and cook over a slow fire without adding water till the potatoes turn soft.

Batatechi bhajee

250 grams potatoes, boiled, peeled and diced. 1 tsp. cumin seeds. Pinch of asafoetida. 3 red chillies. 2 green chillies, minced. ½-inch piece ginger, minced. 1 tsp. ground cumin seeds. 1 tblsp. corriander powder. ½ tsp. garam masala. 2 tblsps. grated coconut. Handful of sliced corriander leaves. Salt to taste.

Heat 2 tblsps. oil and toss in asafoetida and cumin seeds and ginger and green chillies. When the seeds stop popping and ginger turns pink put in the potatoes and fry to a light golden colour. Pound the chillies and put in along with salt and other spices. Mix well and serve decorated with coconut and corriander leaves.

Peanut potatoes

4 medium potatoes, boiled, peeled and diced. 50

grams roasted and pounded peanuts. 1-inch piece ginger, minced. 1 tsp. cumin seeds. 2 tblsps. grated coconut. Handful sliced corriander leaves. 1 tsp. ground cumin seeds. 1 tblsp. corriander powder. ½ tsp. garam masala. Salt and chilli powder to taste.

Heat 2 tblsps. oil and toss in ginger and cumin seeds. When the seeds stop popping and the ginger turns pink, add the potatoes and fry to a nice red colour. Toss in salt and all the spices. Mix thoroughly and remove from fire. Serve decorated with grated coconut and corriander leaves.

Batatechi sukhi bhajee

4 medium potatoes, boiled, peeled and diced. 2 tblsps. grated coconut. Handful of sliced corriander leaves. ¼ tsp. turmeric powder. A few curry leaves. 2 green chillies, minced. A pinch of asafoetida. ¼ tsp. each of mustard and cumin seeds. A big pinch of sugar. 1 tsp. ground cumin seeds. 1 tsp. corriander powder. Salt, lime juice and chilli powder to taste.

Heat 3 tblsps. oil and toss in cumin and mustard seeds and asafoetida, chillies and curry leaves. When the seeds stop popping, add all the spices and salt and fry briefly. Put in the potatoes and fry till they turn a nice golden colour. Add sugar. mix well and remove from fire. Garnish with coconut and corriander leaves and sprinkle lime juice on top before serving.

DELIGHTS FROM MAHARASHTRA 45

Potato curry

250 grams potatoes, peeled and diced. 100 grams shelled green peas. lime-sized ball of tamarind. 20 cashewnuts. ½ dry coconut. 3 red chillies. 5 green chillies. 1-inch piece ginger. 4 flakes garlic. 1 tsp. poppy seeds. Handful of sliced corriander leaves. ½ tsp. turmeric powder. 1 tsp. ground cumin seeds. 1 tsp. corriander powder. Salt to suit the taste.

Cover tamarind with 2 cups of water for 5 minutes then squeeze out the juice. Grind half of the cashewnuts, coconut, chillies, ginger, garlic and poppy seeds to a fine paste. Heat 5 tblsps. oil and fry the ground paste till the oil starts oozing out. Add all the spices and salt. Fry briefly, add potatoes, peas and remaining cashewnuts fry for a few minutes then pour in the tamarind water. Cover and cook till the vegetables are done. Serve hot garnished with corriander leaves.

Potato kheema

250 grams peeled and grated potatoes. 1 tsp. cumin seeds. 4 green chillies, minced. ½ tsp. sugar. ½ cup beaten curds. 25 grams roasted and coarsely pounded groundnuts. Handful of sliced corriander leaves. Salt to taste.

Heat 2 tblsps. ghee and toss in the cumin seeds, when they stop popping, add chillies and potatoes and fry them till they start changing colour. Pour in half cup water and cook till the potatoes are almost done. Put in the curds and groundnuts and continue cooking till the potatoes are cooked and gravy thick. Serve garnished with corriander leaves.

Tomato curry

8 big ripe tomatoes, blanched and sliced. 1 cup thick and 3 cups thin coconut milk. 1-inch piece ginger. 2 big onions, minced. ½ small bunch finely sliced corriander leaves. A few curry leaves. ½ tsp. turmeric powder. 1 tsp. mustard seeds. A pinch asafoetida. Salt and chilli powder to taste. 2 flakes garlic, crushed.

Put tomatoes, thin coconut milk, salt, ginger, turmeric and chilli powder and curry leaves in a vessel and cook till the tomatoes turn very soft. Remove from fire and set aside. In a big vessel heat 2 tblsps. ghee and add asafoetida and mustard, when the seeds stop popping, add garlic and onions and fry till soft and almond coloured, add the tomato curry, mix well and bring to a boil, reduce heat and pour in the thick coconut milk. Mix well and remove from fire. Serve decorated with corriander leaves.

Tamati cha sar

8 big ripe tomatoes, blanched and sliced. 1 cup thick and 3 cups thin coconut milk. 4 green chillies, crushed to a paste. A few curry leaves. 1 tblsp. sugar. 3 flakes crushed garlic. A big handful sliced corriander leaves. ½ tsp. turmeric powder. 1 tsp. cumin seeds. A pinch of asafoetida. Salt and chilli powder to taste. 1-inch piece ginger, minced.

Blend together tomatoes, thin coconut milk, chillies, curry leaves, sugar, ginger, turmeric, salt and chilli powder in a vessel and cook till the tomatoes turn very soft. Remove from fire and set aside. Heat 3 tblsps. ghee and toss in asafoetida and cumin seeds. When the seeds stop popping, put into the sar. Serve decorated with coriander leaves.

Tomato pitla

7 green tomatoes, cut into four pieces each. 1 tblsp. gram flour. 6 green chillies, slitted. $\frac{1}{4}$ tsp. each of mustard and cumin seeds. A pinch of asafoetida. A few grains of fenugreek seeds. Handful of sliced corriander leaves. $\frac{1}{2}$ tsp. turmeric powder. Salt to taste.

Blend gram flour in 1 cup water and set aside. Heat 3 tblsps. oil and toss in mustard, cumin and fenugreek seeds and asafoetida. When the mixture turns red, add turmeric and salt and fry briefly. Put in the tomatoes and chillies and fry till the tomatoes start changing colour. Put in the gram flour mixture. Cover and cook till the tomatoes are cooked and gravy is thick. Serve decorated with corriander leaves.

Tamatichi bhaji

250 grams groundnuts, roasted. 3 medium tomatoes, blanched and sliced. 8 green chillies. 60 grams each of tamarind and jaggery. 1 tsp. garam masala. 1 tsp. ground cumin seeds. Salt and chilli powder to taste. Handful of finely sliced corriander leaves.

Cover tamarind with 1 cup water for 5 minutes, then squeeze out the juice. Put in jaggery and set aside till it dissolves. Grind groundnuts and chillies to a paste. Cook all the above ingredients with the exception of corriander leaves till the bhaji turns thick. Mix well and remove from fire. Garnish with corriander leaves and serve with hot, hot puries, you can also serve this bhaji as an accompaniment to any snack of your choice.

Sweet and sour suran

500 grams yam or suran, peeled and grated. 4 green chillies, minced. Handful sliced corriander leaves. ½-inch piece ginger, minced. ½ tsp. turmeric powder. 1 tsp. sugar. 1 small ball tamarind. A pinch asafoetida. 1 tsp. mustard seeds. 25 grams groundnuts, roasted and pounded coarsely. Salt and chilli powder to taste.

Boil the suran in salted water in which either a teaspoon of lime juice or vinegar has been added till tender. Drain out the water and set aside. Cover tamarind with water for 5 minutes, then squeeze out the juice. Heat 2 tblsps. oil and toss in asafoetida and mustard, when the seeds stop popping, add ginger, green chillies turmeric and salt. When the ginger turns soft, put in the suran and mix well. Put in the rest of the above ingredients with the exception of corriander leaves. Cook till the gravy turns thick. Serve decorated with corriander leaves.

Suran koshumbiri

500 grams suran, peeled and grated. 1 medium onion, minced. 2 green chillies, minced. Handful of sliced corriander leaves. 1 tblsp. grated coconut. Salt to taste.

Sprinkle salt on suran and set aside for 15 minutes, then squeeze out the water. Deep fry suran till crisp and golden. Drain nicely and mix in the rest of the above ingredients.

Suran curry

500 grams suran, peeled and cubed. 100 grams shelled green peas. 1 cup coconut milk. 1 small ball tamarind. Handful sliced corriander leaves. 1 tblsp. corriander powder. 1 tsp. ground cumin seeds. 1 tsp. mustard seeds. ½ tsp. turmeric powder. 1 small onion, minced. 1-inch piece ginger, minced. Salt and chilli powder to taste.

Boil suran in salted water to which a little vinegar or lime juice has been added till tender. Drain out the water and set aside. Cover tamarind with half cup water for 5 minutes, then squeeze out the juice. Heat 2 tblsps. oil and toss in the mustard seeds. When they stop popping, put in the onion and ginger and fry till they change colour. Add peas, all the spices and salt. Mix well then put in the coconut milk. Cover and cook till the peas are almost done, then put in the suran and tamarind and continue cooking till peas are done. Serve decorated with corriander leaves.

Mango curry

6 small ripe mangoes, peeled. ½ coconut, finely grated. A few curry leaves. 1 tsp. garam masala. 4 red chillies. 4 flakes garlic. 1 medium onion. ½ tsp. each of mustard and cumin seeds. 3 green chillies. 1 tblsp. raisins. Salt to taste.

Roast lightly and grind coconut, cumin seeds, garlic, onion and 1 red chilli to a smooth paste. Put mangoes in a pan, put in the chillies and salt and 2 cups water. Cook for 10 minutes, then put in the ground paste mixed with 1 cup water and raisins. Cook for 5 more minutes and remove from fire. Heat 1 tblsp. oil and fry the mustard seeds and remaining red chillies after breaking them into pieces. When the seeds stop popping, pour over the curry. Serve with plain boiled rice.

Mango treat

250 grams raw mangoes, peeled and sliced. 250 grams finely grated jaggery. 1 tsp. each of garam masala and ground cumin seeds. A big pinch of mustard seeds. Pinch of asafoetida. Salt and chilli powder to taste. 2 tblsps. raisins.

Cover jaggery with little water and set aside till it dissolves. Heat 2 tblsps. oil and toss in the mustard and asafoetida. When the seeds stop popping, put in the mangoes and fry till soft. Put in jaggery and rest of the above ingredients and cook till the mangoes are cooked. Serve with hot puries.

Parval and val dalimbi

250 grams parval. 75 grams sprouted val. 2 tblsps. grated coconut. 1 tsp. ground cumin seeds. 1 tblsp. corriander powder. ¼ tsp. mustard seeds. Pinch of asafoetida. ½ tsp. turmeric powder. Handful of sliced corriander leaves. 1 tblsp. grated jaggery. Salt and chilli powder to taste.

To sprout val soak val whole day in water. Drain out the water and tie in a cloth. Hang from a nail in the wall and set aside whole night. By next morning you will see that it has developed sprouts. Peel the beans and set aside. Heat 2 tblsps. oil and add mustard seeds and asafoetida. When the seeds stop popping, add all the spices and fry briefly. Add the val, mix and put 2 cups water and salt. When almost done, add the gourd and jaggery and continue cooking till tender. Serve hot garnished with corriander and coconut.

Parvalchi bhajee

500 grams parval, cut into thin rings. 6 green chillies, minced. 2 tblsps. grated coconut. 1 medium onion, finely sliced. Strained juice of half a lime. Handful of corriander leaves. 1-inch piece ginger, minced. ¼ tsp. turmeric powder. ½ tsp. mustard seeds. Salt, chilli powder and sugar to taste.

Heat 2 tblsps. oil and toss in the mustard, when the seeds stop popping add ginger, onion and chillies and cook till soft. Add turmeric, parval and salt, put in a little water and cook till almost done. Add coconut and sugar and continue cooking till the vegetable is done. Remove from fire, sprinkle lime juice on top and serve garnished with corriander leaves.

Jackfruit treat

1 medium jackfruit. 1 coconut. 1 medium onion, minced. ¼ tsp. turmeric powder. ½ tsp. each of mustard and cumin seeds. 2 tsps. sugar. Handful of sliced corriander leaves. Salt and chilli powder to taste.

Extract 3 cups thin and 1 cup thick milk from coconut. Peel the jackfruit then with oiled fingers separate the fruit and discard the seeds. Apply turmeric to fruit and set aside. Heat 4 tblsps. oil and toss in mustard and cumin seeds, when the seeds stop popping, add onion and fry to almond colour. Add jackfruit, salt and chilli powder, mix nicely and add sugar and thin coconut milk. Cook till the jackfruit is done and gravy thick. Mix in the thick milk and remove from fire. Serve decorated with corriander leaves.

Kela chi bhajee

6 raw bananas, peeled and cubed. 5 green chillies, minced. 2 medium onions, minced. 1 tsp. ground cumin seeds. ½ tsp. mustard seeds. Pinch of asafoetida. Handful of sliced corriander leaves. 2 tblsps. grated coconut. ¼ tsp. turmeric powder. Salt and chilli powder to taste.

Heat 2 tblsps. oil and toss in the asafoetida and mustard. When the seeds burst, add turmeric,

DELIGHTS FROM MAHARASHTRA

salt and bananas and ground cumin seeds. Put in 1 cup water and cook till the bananas are done and gravy is thick. Serve decorated with corriander and coconut.

Moongfali chi ghanti

1 cup peeled and nicely ground groundnuts. 4 green chillies, minced. 1 tblsp. grated coconut. Handful corriander leaves. Strained juice of half a lime. 1 tsp. cumin seeds. $\frac{1}{4}$ tsp. turmeric powder. A pinch of asafoetida. Salt, sugar and chilli powder to taste.

Mix together peanuts, chillies, salt, coconut, sugar and 4 cups water and cook for 5 minutes. Remove from fire and put in corriander leaves. Heat 2 tblsps. ghee and put in asafoetida and cumin seeds, when the seeds stop popping, put into the groundnuts. Serve hot.

Peanut curry

500 grams raw peanuts. 1 tsp. each of poppy, corriander, cumin seeds and til. 2 red chillies. 1 tsp. mango powder. $\frac{1}{4}$ coconut. $\frac{1}{2}$ tsp. turmeric powder. 2 small onions, minced. 1 big tomato, blanched and sliced. 1 tsp. grated jaggery. Handful of corriander leaves. Salt and chilli powder to taste.

Grind together poppy, corriander, cumin seeds and til, chillies and coconut to a fine paste. Heat 3 tblsp. ghee and fry the onions to almond colour, add ground paste and cook till ghee oozes out. Add the nuts, tomato, jaggery and salt.

Cook till the mixture turns dry. Then pour in 2 cups water and cook till the nuts are tender and almost dry. Garnish with corriander leaves and serve with puries.

Buttermilk curry

1 glass sour buttermilk. 1 tblsp. roasted gram flour. 4 flakes garlic. 1 tsp. each of cumin and corriander seeds. 3 green chillies, slitted. A few curry leaves. 1-inch piece ginger, minced. $\frac{1}{2}$ tsp. mustard seeds. A pinch asafoetida. $\frac{1}{4}$ tsp. turmeric powder. 1 tsp. sugar. Salt and chilli powder to taste.

Grind corriander, cumin seeds, ginger and garlic to a paste. Mix together gram flour and buttermilk till smooth. Heat 2 tblsps. ghee and toss in asafoetida and mustard. When the seeds stop popping, add ginger paste and fry briefly. Add curry leaves chillies, sugar and all the spices, salt and buttermilk. Bring slowly to a boil and remove from fire. Serve decorated with sliced corriander leaves.

Cocum curry

6 cocums. 1 cup coconut milk. 2 tsps. sugar. 1 tsp. cumin seeds. $\frac{1}{4}$ tsp. turmeric powder. Handful sliced corriander leaves. 2 green chillies, slitted. Salt and chilli powder to taste.

Wash the cocums nicely. Heat 2 tblsps. ghee and put in the cumin seeds. When they stop popping, add cocums, 1 cup water along with the rest of the above ingredients with the exception of coconut milk. When the cocums turn soft.

put in the coconut milk, mix well and remove from fire. Serve with plain boiled rice.

Vada curry

2 cloves. 1-inch piece cinnamon stick, broken into bits. 1 small bay leaf, crumpled. A few cardamom seeds. ½ tsp. turmeric powder. 3 cups thin and 1 cup thick coconut milk. Handful of sliced corriander leaves. 4 green chillies, slitted. 4 cocums. 2 medium onions. ¼ coconut. 4 flakes garlic. 1-inch piece ginger. Salt to taste.

For vadas......2 cups gram flour. ¼ cup broken rice. 4 flakes garlic. 1-inch piece ginger. 1 tsp. ground cumin seeds. 1 tblsp. corriander powder. 2 green chillies. Handful of corriander leaves. Salt to taste.

Grind coarsely ginger, garlic, chillies and corriander leaves. Heat 2 tblsps. ghee and put in 3 cups water and ground ginger paste, gram flour and rice. Cook stirring all the time till the mixture turns thick and leaves the sides of the vessel. Remove from fire and put in a greased thali. Set aside to turn cold, then cut into cubes and deep fry to a golden brown colour. Drain and set aside. Fry coconut and onion to a red colour and grind to a fine paste. Wash the cocums nicely in water. Grind ginger and garlic. Heat 3 tblsps. oil and put in the whole spices, then put in ginger and coconut paste and cook till the oil oozes out. Put in salt, turmeric, chillies, cocums and thin coconut milk and cook till the cocums are tender. Put in the vadas and simmer for 5 minutes. Pour in the thick coconut milk and mix well. Serve decorated with corriander leaves.

Coconut curry

3 cups thin and 1 cup thick coconut milk. 150 grams ripe tomatoes, peeled and blanched. 4 red chillies. A pinch asafoetida. Few curry leaves. ¼ tsp. each of mustard and cumin seeds. Handful of sliced corriander leaves. 1 tsp. gram flour. 1 tblsp. grated coconut. 4 flakes garlic. 1-inch piece ginger. 2 medium onions. 2 green chillies, slitted. Salt to taste.

Blend gram flour in thin coconut milk. Grind onions, ginger and garlic coarsely. Soak red chillies in ¼ cup hot water for half an hour, then mash to a fine paste. Heat 3 tblsps. ghee and toss in asafoetida, mustard and cumin seeds. When the seeds stop popping, put in the onion paste and coconut and fry to almound colour. Put in thin coconut milk and whole chillies and tomatoes and red chilli water and cook till the tomatoes turn soft. Add thick coconut milk, mix nicely and remove from fire. Garnish with corriander leaves and serve with plain boiled rice.

Sago khichdi

250 grams sago. 250 grams roasted and pounded groundnuts, ½ tsp. cumin seeds. 4 green chillies, minced. ½ tsp. sugar. Handful sliced corriander leaves. Salt to taste. 2 tblsps. grated coconut.

DELIGHTS FROM MAHARASHTRA

Wash sago and drain the water, then set aside for half an hour. Heat 2 tblsps. ghee and add cumin seeds and chillies. When the seeds burst add the rest of the above ingredients with the exception of coconut and corriander leaves. Cover tightly, sprinkle little water over lid and cook without adding water till the sago is cooked. Serve garnished with coconut and corriander leaves.

Plain pitla

Plain pitla. 1 cup gram flour. 2 small onions. 2 flakes garlic. 4 green chillies. ½ cup grated coconut. 2 tblsps. tamarind juice. A big pinch mustard seeds. 1 tsp. garam masala. Handful corriander leaves. Salt and chilli powder to taste.

Grind onion, garlic, chillies and coconut to a coarse paste. Heat 4 tblsps. ghee and fry mustard till it bursts, put in the coconut paste and fry to almond colour. Add gram flour and fry to a nice red colour. Add 2 cups water, spices, salt and tamrind and cook stirring all the time till the mixture turns thick and dry. Serve with puries garnished with corriander leaves.

Panchamrut No. 1

100 grams raw peanuts. 50 grams cashewnuts. ½ dry coconut. 4 tblsps. til. 1 lime-sized ball of tamarind. 25 grams grated jaggery. ¼ tsp. mustard seeds. Pinch of asafoetida. ¼ tsp. turmeric powder. ½ tsp. ground cumin seeds. ½ tsp. garam masala. 6 dates, pitted and sliced finely. 2 tblsps. sliced raisins. Salt and chilli powder to taste.

Roast 25 grams of peanuts and pound it coarsely. Soak the remaining peanuts in water for 1 hour and peel them. Chop cashewnuts, dice the coconut. Roast til and pound them. Cover tamarind with 2 cups water for 5 minutes and extract juice. Heat 3 tblsps. ghee and add mustard and asafoetida, when the seeds stop popping, add cashewnuts, peanuts and coconut and fry for 5 minutes. Add the rest of the above ingredients and cook over a slow fire till the panchamrut turns thick. Serve hot.

Panchamrut No. 2

½ dry coconut. 25 grams peanuts. 1 marble-sized ball of tamarind. 2 cups coconut milk. 6 long, thick green chillies, sliced. 1 tsp. garam masala. 3 tblsps. grated jaggery. 2 tblsps. sliced cashewnuts. 2 tblsps. raisins. 25 grams cashewnuts. Salt to taste. 2 tblsps. sliced coconut.

Fry cashewnuts, sliced coconut and raisins. Fry dry coconut with peanuts to a red colour and grind to a paste along with tamarind and jaggery. Heat coconut milk add chillies and ground paste, salt and garam masala and cook till the chillies turn soft. Remove from fire and serve garnished with sliced and fried coconut, cashewnuts and raisins.

Poha bhajee

250 grams poha or beaten rice. 75 grams each of peas and tomatoes. 1 medium potato, peeled and cubed. 2 green chillies, minced. Pinch asafoetida. ¼ tsp. mustard seeds. ½ tsp. turmeric

powder. 2 tblsps. grated coconut. Handful of sliced corriander leaves. Salt, chilli powder and lime juice to taste. 1 medium onion, minced.

Wash poha nicely in water and set aside. Heat 2 tblsps. ghee and add asafoetida and mustard. When the seeds burst, add turmeric, salt, peas, potatoes and tomatoes. Cover tightly and cook without adding water till the vegetables are done. Heat 2 tblsps. ghee in a separate vessel and fry onions and chillies till soft, add poha and cooked vegetables and cook till poha turns soft and not soggy. Remove from fire and sprinkle lime juice on top. Serve garnished with coconut and corriander leaves.

Batata poha

250 grams potatoes, peeled and cubed. 250 grams poha. 25 grams sago. 25 grams roasted peanuts. Handful of sliced corriander leaves. 2 green chillies, minced. $\frac{1}{2}$-inch piece ginger, minced. 2 tblsps. grated coconut. $\frac{1}{4}$ tsp. mustard seeds. $\frac{1}{4}$ tsp. cumin seeds. $\frac{1}{4}$ tsp. turmeric powder. 1 tsp. sugar. $\frac{1}{2}$ cup milk. 1 medium onion, minced. A few curry leaves. A pinch asafoetida. Salt, chilli powder and lime to taste.

Soak sago in water for a few hours, drain out the water and set aside. Wash and soak poha in milk. Powder peanuts. Heat 3 tblsps. oil and toss in mustard, cumin and asafoetida. When the seeds stop popping, add turmeric ginger, onion and chillies and fry till soft, add potatoes, curry leaves and salt and fry for 5 minutes. Add sago. Cover tightly and cook without adding water till the potatoes and sago are cooked. Put in poha, mix well and continue cooking till the poha turns soft but not soggy. Remove from fire and sprinkle lime juice on top. Serve decorated with corriander leaves and coconut.

Khaman poha

500 grams poha. ½ coconut, finely grated. Handful corriander leaves. 100 grams onions, minced. 1 tsp. sugar. 1-inch piece ginger, minced. 2 green chillies, minced. ¼ tsp. turmeric powder. ¼ tsp. each of cumin and mustard seeds. A few curry leaves. Pinch of asafoetida. Salt and chilli powder to taste. Strained juice of 1 lime.

Wash poha nicely in water. Heat 3 tblsps. oil and toss in cumin and mustard and asafoetida. When the seeds stop popping, put in ginger, onions chillies and curry leaves and cook till soft. Add all the above ingredients with the exception of corriander leaves and cook without adding water till the poha turns soft. Serve decorated with corriander leaves.

Pohebhat

250 grams poha. 2 medium onions, minced. 5 green chillies, minced. 1-inch piece ginger, minced. ¼ coconut, finely grated. Handful sliced corriander leaves. ¼ tsp. turmeric powder. 3 flakes garlic. A few curry leaves. 1 tsp. sugar. Juice of 1 lime. ½ tsp. mustard seeds. Salt and chilli powder to taste. A pinch of asafoetida. 150 grams shelled green peas. ¼ tsp. cumin seeds. 1 big potato, peeled and diced.

Wash the poha nicely in water and squeeze out the water. Heat 3 tblsps. oil and toss in asafoetida, mustard and cumin seeds. When the seeds stop popping. Add garlic, ginger, chillies, onions and curry leaves and fry till soft. Put in turmeric, salt and vegetables. Cover tightly and cook without adding water till the vegetables are done. Put in poha, lime juice and coconut and continue cooking till the poha turns soft. Serve decorated with corriander leaves.

Koal poha

1 cup poha. 1 cup coconut milk. $\frac{1}{4}$ cup tamarind juice. $\frac{1}{2}$ tsp. cumin seeds. 1 chilli. 1 big handful corriander leaves. 2 tblsps. sugar. Salt and chilli powder to taste.

Wash the poha and squeeze out the water. Mix together coconut milk, tamarind and poha and sugar. Grind chilli and corriander leaves and mix in. Heat 1 tblsp. ghee and toss in cumin seeds, when they stop popping, put into the poha.

DELIGHTS FROM MAHARASHTRA

With the poha, pour in water and knead out into layer. Place 3 tablespoons and toss in curry leaves, mustard and cumin seeds. When the seeds stop popping. Add garlic, green chillies, onion and curry leaves, and fry till soft. Put in turmeric, salt and vegetables. Cover tightly and cook with out adding water till the vegetables are done. Put in poha, lime juice and coconut, and continue cooking till the poha turns soft. Serve decorated with coriander leaves.

Koal poha

1 1/2 cup poha, 1 cup coconut milk, 1 cup tamarind juice, 1 tsp cumin seeds, 1 chilli, 1 big handful coriander leaves, 2 tbsp sugar, Salt and chilli powder to also.

Wash the poha and squeeze out the water. Mix together coconut milk, tamarind and poha, and sugar. Grind chilli and coriander leaves, and mix into this. Heat ghee and toss in cumin seeds. When they stop popping, put into the poha.

PICKLES AND CHUTNEYS

Hot mango pickle

1 kilo raw mangoes. 25 grams mustard seeds. 1 tsp. asafoetida. 25 grams chilli powder. 2 tblsps. turmeric powder. 500 grams oil. Salt.

Wash and cut mangoes into small pieces. Sprinkle on them salt and turmeric powder and set aside for 6 hours. Heat oil till blue smoke rises from its surface and toss in the asafoetida and mustard seeds, when they stop popping, remove from fire, cool and mix in chilli powder. Squeeze out water from mangoes and put them in a clean jar and then pour oil on top. Keep aside for 6 days before using it.

Guramba

1 kilo raw mangoes. ½ kilo finely grated jaggery. 125 grams oil. 2 tblsps. turmeric powder. ½ tsp. asafoetida. 2 tblsps. each of ground cumin seeds and chilli powder. 4 cloves. 1-inch piece cinnamon stick, 1 bay leaf. Salt to taste.

Wash and cut mangoes into small pieces. Apply salt and turmeric on them and set aside for 6 hours, then squeeze out the water. Coarsely pound all the whole spices. Mix jaggery into oil and keep on stirring till it dissolves into the oil. Mix in the rest of the above ingredients and store in a clean jar. Set aside for 8 days before using it.

Sweet and sour mango pickle

1 kilo raw mangoes, peeled and grated. 25 grams mustard seeds. 1 cup sugar. 1 tblsp. turmeric powder. 25 grams chilli powder. 1 tblsp. ground cumin seeds. 5 cloves. 2-inch piece cinnamon stick. 250 grams oil. Salt.

Powder coarsely whole cloves and cinnamon coarsely. Apply salt and turmeric on mangoes and set aside for 6 hours, then squeeze out the water. Heat oil till blue smoke rises from its surface, then toss in asafoetida and mustard. When the seeds stop popping, put in the rest of the spices, mix well and remove from fire. Cool the oil and mix in the mangoes and sugar. Put in a clean jar and set aside for 4 days.

Mango murraba

1 kilo raw mangoes, peeled and grated. ½ kilo sugar. 1 tblsp. cardamom seeds. 1-inch piece cinnamon stick, broken into bits. 25 grams blanched and sliced almonds and pistachios. 1 tblsp charoli. A few drops essence of kewda or rose. Salt.

Apply salt on mangoes and set aside for a few hours, then squeeze out the water. Put 2 cups of water in sugar and prepare a syrup of one-thread consistency. Put in the mangoes and cook over a slow fire till the mangoes are tender and syrup thick. Remove from fire cool and mix in the remaining ingredients and store in airtight bottle.

Hot lime pickle

20 limes. 25 grams mustard seeds. 25 grams chilli powder. 2 tblsps. turmeric powder. 1 cup sugar. 1 tblsp. fenugreek seeds. 5 cloves. 2-inch piece cinnamon stick. 250 grams oil.

Wash and cut the limes into four halfway through. Pound together fenugreek seeds, cloves mustard seeds and cinnamon. Mix together all the spices, salt and sugar and stuff into the lime.

Heat oil till blue smoke rises from its surface, cool and pour over the limes. Set aside for 15 days before using it.

Amla murraba

1 kilo amlas. 1 kilo sugar. 1 tblsp. cardamom seeds. A few drops either essence of saffron, kewda or rose. ¼ tsp. pan-ka-chuna. ¼ tsp. ground alum. Silver or gold foil.

Poke holes into each amla with a sharp needle. Dissolve alum and chuna in 2 litres water put in amlas and set aside for half an hour. Drain out the water and wash in 3 to 4 changes of water. Boil the amlas till they turn tender. Drain out the water and put in a dekchi along with sugar and cardamom seeds. Keep on a slow fire till the syrup becomes thick, but do not allow the syrup to become too thick as it will thicken even more when cool. Remove from fire, sprinkle essence over them. Cover with foil, cool and bottle.

Amla pickle

1 kilo amlas. 250 grams oil. 25 grams each of mustard seeds and chilli powder. 1 tblsp. turmeric powder. 1 tblsp. each of fenugreek and cumin seeds. 5 cloves. 2-inch piece cinnamon stick. Salt. 2 tblsps. sugar. ¼ tsp. pan-ka-chuna. ¼ tsp. ground alum.

Poke holes into each amla with a sharp needle. Dissolve alum and chuna in 2 litres water and toss in the amlas. Set aside for 30 minutes, drain out the water and wash in 3 to 4 changes of clear water, then cut into fours halfway through. Powder all the whole spices together, mix in the remaining ingredients and stuff into the amlas. Heat oil till blue smoke rises from its surface. Cool and pour over the amlas. Set aside for 1 week.

Carrot pickle

1 kilo carrots, peel and cut into thin long pieces. 25 grams mustard seeds. 1 tblsp. each of fenugreek seeds, cumin seeds and turmeric powder. 2 tblsps. each of chilli powder and sugar. 5 cloves. 2-inch piece cinnamon stick. 100 grams oil. Salt.

Powder together all the spices. Apply salt on carrots and set aside for a few hours, then squeeze out all the water. Heat oil till smoke rises from its surface, put in all the spices, fry briefly then remove from fire. Cool and mix in the carrots and sugar. Put in airtight bottle and set aside for 4 days.

Carrot murraba

1 kilo carrots, peeled and cut into thin slices. 500 grams sugar. 1 tblsp. cardamom seeds. 1 tsp. essence of saffron or kewda or rose. Silver or gold foil.

Poke holes in to the carrot pieces nicely with a needle. Boil in water till almost tender. Drain completely and dry for a few hours. Put 2 cups sugar in water and prepare a syrup of one-thread consistency. Put in the carrots and cardamoms and cook over a slow fire till the syrup turns thick. Remove from fire, sprinkle essence on top, cover with pieces of foil and store in airtight bottle after cooling it.

Chilli pickle

1 kilo small and thick green chillies. 2 tblsps. fenugreek seeds. 4 tblsps. salt. 50 grams mustard seeds. 1 tsp. asafoetida. 5 cloves. 2-inch piece cinnamon stick. 2 tblsps. sugar. 400 grams oil.

Powder together all the whole spices. Make a slit halfway through into each chilli and stuff with spices, sugar and salt. Heat oil till blue smoke rises from its surface. Cool and put into the chillies. Set aside for 4 days before using it.

Prawn pickle

500 grams prawns, cleaned and shelled. 2 medium onions, minced. 6 tblsps thick tamarind juice. 12 red chillies. 1 tsp. turmeric powder. 2 tblsps. corriander seeds. Salt. 1 tblsp. garam masala.

Do not wash prawns in water but vinegar. If you will use water the pickle will not last. Powder together all the whole spices after roasting them. Heat 5 tblsps. oil and fry the onions to a pale golden till dry. Pour tamarind juice and spices over top. Cover tightly and cook till the prawns are done. Remove from fire, cool and put in airtight bottle. Instead of prawns you can pickle bangda in the same way. This pickle lasts for 1 month.

Bhopla skin chutney

1 cup skin of red bhopla. 4 green chillies. Handful of corriander leaves. ¼ coconut. 25 grams roasted groundnuts. 1 tblsp. til or sesame seeds. lime juice and salt to taste.

Fry the skins nicely in ghee or oil and then grind to a paste with all the above ingredients using a little water.

Chutney of curry leaves

1 small bunch curry leaves. 2 tblsps. roasted til or sesame seeds. 4 red chillies. Salt and sugar to taste.

Fry the leaves in oil till crisp. Drain, cool and pound to a powder with the rest of the above ingredients. Store in airtight container and use when required.

Lasun chi tikhat

2 pods garlic. 1 dry coconut. 1 tblsp. cumin seeds. 6 red chillies. 2 tblsps. sesame seeds or til. 1 lime-sized ball of tamarind. 12 groundnuts. Salt.

Roast all the above ingredients to a red colour on a girdle and then pound to a coarse paste. Store in airtight bottle and use when required. This lasts for 15 to 20 days.

Chilli chutney

8 thick and long green chillies. 5 flakes garlic. 1 tblsp. sugar. ¼ coconut. ½ lime. 1 bunch corriander leaves. Salt to taste.

Grind all the above ingredients to a fine paste with little water, then mix in lime juice.

Peanut chutney

25 grams roasted peanuts. Strained juice of half a lime. 2 green chillies. 1 tsp. sugar. Salt to taste. Grind all the above ingredients to a paste with very little water.

Coconut chutney

$\frac{1}{4}$ coconut. Juice of 1 lime. 1 tsp. sugar. 6 green chillies. 1-inch pieceginger. 4 flakes garlic. 1 bunch corriander leaves. $\frac{1}{4}$ tsp. turmeric powder 1 tsp. cumin seeds. Salt to taste.

Grind all the above ingredients to a paste with very little water.

PULSES & LENTILS

Masurchi amti

250 grams whole masur dal. ½ dry coconut. 100 grams roasted peanuts without skins. 25 grams finely grated jaggery. 1 lime-sized ball of tamarind. 1 tblsp. garam masala. Handful of sliced corriander leaves. Salt and chilli powder to taste. ½ tsp. turmeric powder.

Grind coconut to a paste after frying it in oil to a red colour. Powder the peanuts coarsely. Soak tamarind in half cup water for 5 minutes, then squeeze out the pulp. Boil the dal in water to which turmeric has been added till nearly done, then put in the coconut paste, peanuts, tamarind and jaggery and salt. When the dal is cooked mix well and remove from fire. Heat 2 tblsps. ghee and put in garam masala and chilli powder, fry briefly and pour over the dal. Serve garnished with corriander leaves.

Katachi amti

1 cup channa dal. 50 grams peanuts. 1 small ball tamrind. A pinch of asafoetida. 1 tsp. gram flour. ½ tsp. turmeric powder. 1 tsp. garam masala. Handful of corriander leaves. 1 tblsp. grated jaggery. Salt and chilli powder to taste.

Roast peanuts and powder them coarsely. Cover tamarind with half cup water for 5 minutes and then squeeze out the pulp. Cook dal in water to which turmeric has been added until it turns almost tender, then put in peanuts, tamarind, jaggery and salt and continue cooking till the dal is done. Heat 2 tblsps. ghee and fry gram flour to a red colour, put in garam masala and chilli powder, mix well and put into the dal. Mix nicely and serve decorated with corriander leaves.

Dal channa

1 cup channa dal. 1 medium onion, minced. Handful of sliced corriander leaves. ¼ dry coconut. 3 green chillies. 1 tsp. each of mustard and cumin seeds. ½ tsp. turmeric powder. A few curry leaves. A pinch asafoetida. Salt and chilli powder to taste.

Soak the dal whole night in water. Next morning, drain out the water and grind it coarsely. Fry the coconut and grind it to a paste. Heat 3 tblsps. oil and toss in cumin and mustard seeds and asafoetida, when the seeds stop popping, put in the onion and curry leaves and chillies and cook till soft. Put in the dal along with turmeric, salt, chilli powder, coconut and ½ cup water. Cover and cook till the dal turns tender and dry. Serve decorated with corriander leaves.

Dal toovar

2 cups toovar dal. 1 bunch fenugreek leaves. 25 grams raw peanuts. 1 small ball tamarind. 4 green chillies, minced. Handful of corriander leaves. 1 tblsp. grated jaggery. 1 tsp. garam masala. 1 tsp. mustard seeds. ½ tsp. turmeric powder. A pinch asafoetida. 1 tblsp. grated coconut. Salt and chilli powder to taste.

Soak peanuts in water for half an hour. Drain out the water and remove peels. Cover tamarind with water for 5 minutes, then squeeze out the pulp. Wash and soak dal in water for a few hours. Sprinkle fenugreek leaves with salt for 15 minutes, then squeeze out the water to remove bitterness. Put in fenugreek leaves and peanuts into the dal along with turmeric and cook till the dal is almost done. Put in salt, chillies, tamarind, jaggery and chilli powder and continue cooking till the dal turns tender. Remove from fire and set aside. Heat 2 tblsps. ghee and put in asafoetida and mustard, when the seeds stop popping, put in the garam masala and pour over the dal. Serve decorated with grated coconut and corriander leaves.

Whole moong

2 cups whole moong dal. 5 chillies, minced. 1-inch piece ginger, minced. 1 medium onion, minced. 1 tsp. ground cumin seeds. 1 tblsp. corriander powder. A pinch asafoetida. Handful of corriander leaves. 3 cups thin and 1 cup thick coconut milk. Salt, chilli powder and lime juice to taste.

Soak the dal in water for 24 hours, drain out the water and the dal in a piece of muslin. Hang up the bag of muslin from a nail in the wall whole night. Next morning, remove the dal from cloth and you will find that it has developed sprouts. Heat 2 tblsps. oil and fry asafoetida chillies, ginger and onion till soft. Add all the spices, dal, corriander leaves, salt and thin coconut milk and continue cooking till the dal is almost done. Pour in thick coconut milk. Remove from fire when the dal is tender and quite dry. Sprinkle lime juice on top before serving.

Spicy toovar dal

2 cups toovar dal. 1 tsp. ground cumin seeds. 1 tblsp. corriander seeds 4 green chillies, slitted. 4 cocums. 1 tsp. mustard seeds. 2 tblsps. grated coconut. 1 big tomato, blanched and sliced. $\frac{1}{4}$ tsp. turmeric powder. Handful of corriander leaves. 1-inch piece ginger, minced. Salt to taste.

Wash the cocums nicely in water. Boil the dal with turmeric in water till almost done, then put in the tomatoes, chillies, cocums, coconut, salt and all the spices and continue cooking till the dal is tender. Remove from fire and set aside. Heat 2 tblsps. oil and toss in mustard, when the mustard stops popping, put in the ginger and fry till it turns pink, then pour into the dal. Serve decorated with corriander leaves.

Varan

1 cup toovar dal $\frac{1}{2}$ tsp. turmeric powder. Salt. 1 small onion, minced. 1-inch piece ginger, minced. 1 small tomato, sliced. 1 tblsp. grated coconut. Handful of sliced corriander leaves. 1 tsp. cumin seeds.

Boil dal in water to which turmeric has been added till tender and quite dry. Mix in salt and cook for a few more minutes. Remove from fire and mash to a thickpaste. Heat 2 tblsps. ghee add cumin and fry till they pop and add the remaining ingredients and fry for a few minutes. Put over the dal before serving.

DELIGHTS FROM MAHARASHTRA

Dal moong

125 grams whole moong. 75 grams baby onions, peeled. ½ tsp. turmeric powder. 2 tblsps. tamarind juice. Handful of sliced corriander leaves. 1-inch piece ginger, minced. 4 green chillies, minced. 1 tblsp. grated coconut. Salt and chilli powder to taste. 1 tsp. cumin seeds.

Soak dal whole night in water. Next morning, drain out the water. Fry onions in oil till they start changing colour. Heat 1 tblsp. oil and fry ginger and chillies till soft, add dal and turmeric and cover with water. Cook till the dal is almost done. Put in the onions and tamarind and salt and continue cooking till the dal and the onions are done. Remove from fire and sprinkle on top coconut and corriander leaves. Heat 1 tblsp. oil and toss in cumin seeds and a pinch of asafoetida. When the seeds stop popping, put over the dal. Serve hot.

Sprouted beans

250 grams dried white beans, 2 medium onions, minced. 4 flakes garlic, minced. 4 green chillies. 1 piece ginger. 1 tsp. cumin seeds. 1 tsp. corriander seeds. ½ tsp. turmeric powder. A pinch of asafoetida. 2 cups coconut milk. 4 cocums. 1 tblsp. grated jaggery. Handful of corriander leaves. Salt to taste.

Wash the cocums nicely in water. Sprout the beans in the same way as shown in the recipe entitled whole moong. Grind together garlic, chillies, ginger, corriander and cumin seeds. Heat 2 tblsps. oil and fry onions till soft. Add asafoetida ground paste and fry nicely. Put in the turmeric and beans. Mix well, pour in the coconut milk and cook over a slow fire till the beans are almost done. Add cocums, salt and jaggery and continue cooking till the beans are done. Serve garnished with corriander leaves.

Usal

125 grams dried white beans. 100 grams onions, minced. $\frac{1}{2}$ tsp. turmeric powder. $\frac{1}{4}$ tsp. mustard seeds. A pinch asafoetida. 1 lime-sized ball of tamarind. 1 tblsp. grated jaggery. 2 tblsps. grated coconut. 4 green chillies, minced. 1 tsp. ground cumin seeds. 1 tblsp. corriander powder. 4 flakes garlic. 1-inch piece ginger. Salt to suit the taste.

Wash and soak beans whole night in water. Next morning, boil them in the same water in which they were soaked along with turmeric, green chillies and all the spices till soft. Remove from fire and set aside. Cover tamarind with water for 5 minutes, then squeeze out the juice. Heat 3 tblsps. oil and toss in asafoetida and mustard. When the seeds stop popping, put in ground onions ginger and garlic and fry to a rich golden colour. Put in salt and boiled beans, tamarind and jaggery and cook for 5 minutes. Serve garnished with coconut and corriander leaves.

Sukhi chawli

500 grams sukhi chawli. $\frac{1}{2}$ grated coconut. 2 medium onions, minced. 3 green chillies, minced. Pinch of asafoetida. $\frac{1}{2}$ tsp. turmeric powder. 1 tsp.

mustard seeds. Handful of corriander leaves. Salt, chilli powder and lime juice to taste.

Soak the chawli whole night in water. Next morning boil it in the water in which it was soaked along with turmeric powder till done. Heat 2 tblsps. oil and toss in asafoetida and mustard. When the seeds stop popping, add onions and chillies and salt and fry till the onions start changing colour. And chawli and coconut. Mix well and cook for five minutes over low fire. Remove from fire, sprinkle lime juice over top and serve decorated with corriander leaves.

FISH & EGGS

Stuffed pomfret

1 medium-sized pomfret. ¼ coconut. 4 green chillies. 1-inch piece ginger. 4 flakes garlic. ½ small bunch corriander leaves. 1 tsp. each of lime juice and sugar. 1 tsp. ground cumin seeds. ½ tsp. turmeric powder. 1 hard-boiled egg, shelled and sliced into thin rings. Salt and chilli powder to taste.

Remove the head and tail of pomfret. Clean nicely and wash in water. Slit the fish halfway through on one side and remove the insides. Wash once again then remove fishy smell...... see helpful hints. Grind all the above ingredients to a fine paste with the exception of eggs and stuff it into the pomfret. Arrange egg slices over the chutney and tie with thread. Shallow fry the pomfret to a golden brown colour. Remove from fire, remove the thread and cut into thick slices. Serve piping hot.

Fish in masala

1 medium pomfret, cleaned and sliced. 2 big onions, sliced into thin rings. 2 tblsps. grated coconut. 2 medium tomatoes, blanched and sliced ½ tsp. turmeric powder. 1 tsp. each of corriander powder and garam masala. 1-inch piece ginger. Handful of sliced corriander leaves. 4 flakes garlic. Salt and chilli powder to taste.

Remove fishy smell of fish......see helpful hints. Grind ginger, garlic and coconut and 4 green chillies to a paste. Heat 4 tblsps. oil and fry the paste along with onions nicely. Put in all the spices and fry briefly. Add fish, fry for a few minutes, then put in tomatoes. Cover tightly and cook till the fish is done. Serve decorated with corriander leaves.

Fried pakoda pomfret

1 medium pomfret. 2-inch piece ginger. 4 flakes garlic. 4 tblsps. gram flour. 1 tsp. lime juice. ½ tsp. turmeric powder. A pinch soda. Salt to taste.

For chutney......¼ coconut. 4 green chillies. A small piece ginger. 2 flakes garlic. ½ small bunch corriander leaves. A few mint leaves. 1 tsp. each of lime juice and sugar. 1 tsp. ground cumin seeds.

Grind all the chutney ingredients to a smooth paste. Mix together gram flour, salt, turmeric and soda, then put in enough water to form a thin batter. Remove the head and tail of fish. Clean nicely and wash in water. Slit it halfway through on one side and with the help of a sharp knife remove the middle bone. Remove fishy smell......see Helpful Hints. Grind ginger and garlic to a paste. Mix with salt, lime juice, garam masala and chilli powder and apply on the body of the fish. Set aside for half an hour, then stuff the chutney into the fish, cover with prepared batter and shallow fry to a golden colour. Drain and serve piping hot.

Spicy pomfret curry

1 pomfret, clean and cut into slices. ¼ coconut. 4 green chillies. 1-inch piece ginger. 4 flakes garlic. ½ small bunch corriander leaves. ½ tsp. turmeric powder. 1 small ball tamarind. 1 tsp.

ground cumin seeds. Salt and chilli powder to taste.

Remove fishy smell of fish......see Helpful Hints. Soak tamarind in 1½ cups water for 5 minutes, then squeeze out the juice. Grind the remaining ingredients to a paste and apply on fish. Heat 4 tblsps. oil and fry the fish nicely, then pour in the tamarind water and cook till the fish is tender. Serve hot with plain boiled rice.

Fish and potato curry

1 medium pomfret, cleaned and sliced. 2 medium potatoes, peeled and diced into cubes. 1 big onion, minced. ½ tsp. turmeric powder. 1 tsp. each of corriander powder and ground cumin seeds. ¼ coconut. 2 big tomatoes, blanched and sliced. 4 green chillies, slitted. A few curry leaves. 2 tblsps. tamarind water. Salt and chilli powder to taste.

Remove fishy smell from fish......see Helpful Hints. Grind coconut to a paste. Heat 4 tblsps. oil and fry the onions till soft. Add coconut and green chillies and fry for five minutes. Add all the spices and fry briefly. Add potatoes, fry for a few minutes, then add tomatoes. Cook till the tomatoes turn soft. Pour in 2 cups water and cook till the potatoes are half done. Put in fish, curry leaves and tamarind water and continue cooking till the fish and the potatoes are done. Serve with plain boiled rice after garnishing with corriander leaves.

Special pomfret curry

1 medium pomfret...cleaned and sliced. 4 green chillies, minced. 1 tblsp. corriander seeds. 2 red chillies. 1-inch piece ginger. 4 flakes garlic. Handful of corriander leaves. ½ tsp. turmeric powder ¼ coconut, 1 big onion, minced. 1 small ball tamarind. Salt and chilli powder to taste.

Remove fishy smell from fish......see Helpful Hints, then fry lightly in oil and set aside. Soak tamarind in 2 cups water for 5 minutes then squeeze out the juice. Grind coconut, red chillies, garlic, corriander seeds and ginger to a paste. Slit green chillies. Heat 3 tblsps. oil and fry the onions till soft, add ground paste and all the spices and salt and fry nicely till a nice smell comes out of the masala. Add fish and tamarind juice and cook till the fish is done. Serve garnished with corriander leaves.

Pomfret masaledar

1 big pomfret, cleaned and sliced. 2 medium onions, minced. ½ coconut. 4 green chillies. ½ tsp. turmeric powder. 8 flakes garlic. 1 tsp. each of cumin and poppy seeds and corriander seeds. 1 small ball tamarind. Salt and chilli powder to taste.

Remove fishy smell from pomfret......see Helpful Hints. Grind coconut, cumin seeds, garlic, ginger, green chillies, corriander and poppy seeds to a paste. Heat 4 tblsps. oil and fry the onions till soft. Add the ground paste fried, soak tamarind in 2 cups water for 5 minutes and then squeeze out the juice. Put the fish into the fried masala, mix well and then pour in the tamarind juice, cook till the fish is tender. Serve decorated with corriander leaves.

Hot and spicy pomfret

1 pomfret, cleaned and cut into slices. 12 flakes garlic. 4 green chillies. 1-inch piece ginger. 1 small ball tamarind. ½ small bunch corriander leaves. 1 tsp. ground cumin seeds. 1 tsp. corriander powder. ¼ coconut, finely grated. Salt and chilli powder to taste.

Remove fishy smell from fish......see Helpful Hints. Grind garlic, chillies, ginger, tamarind and corriander leaves to a paste. Mix in the spices and apply on the slices of fish. Set aside for 15 minutes. Heat 6 tblsps. oil and fry the fish to a red colour. Put in and cook till the fish is almost done. Add the coconut and continue cooking till the fish is done. Serve decorated with corriander leaves.

Fried pomfret

1 medium pomfret, cleaned and sliced into thin slices. 10 flakes garlic. A piece of ginger. ½ cup thick tamarind water. ½ tsp. turmeric powder. 1 tsp. ground cumin seeds. Rice flour. Salt and chilli powder to taste.

Remove fishy smell from fish......see Helpful Hints. Grind ginger, garlic to a paste and mix into the tamarind water along with salt and all the spices. Apply nicely on each slice of fish and set aside for 15 minutes. Roll nicely in rice flour and shallow fry till crisp and golden. Drain and serve piping hot.

Masaledar mackerel

3 bangadas or mackerel. 6 red chillies. $\frac{1}{2}$ cup tamarind juice. 6 red chillies. 6 flakes garlic. 1 tsp. cumin seeds. 1-inch piece ginger. Salt and chilli powder to taste.

Scrape, clean and gut the fishes. Remove fishy smell......see Helpful Hints. Cut into slices. Grind garlic, chillies, cumin seeds and ginger to a paste and apply on the fishes along with tamarind, salt and chilli powder. Heat 4 tblsps. oil and fry the fish. In the begining the fish will give out a lot of water, but go on frying till the pieces turn crisp and golden. Serve hot.

Bombay duck kababs

6 large Bombay ducks. 1-inch piece ginger. 1 medium onion. 6 flakes garlic. 4 green chillies. $\frac{1}{2}$ small bunch corriander leaves. $\frac{1}{2}$ tsp. turmeric powder. 1 tsp. ground cumin seeds. Salt and chilli powder to taste. 2 tblsps. rice flour.

Cut open the fishes lengthwise and take out the middle-bone. Wash them nicely and set aside. Grind the remaining ingredients with the exception of rice flour to a paste. Stuff the ground paste into each fish. Roll nicely in flour and shallow fry till crisp and brown. Serve piping hot.

Bangda curry

1 dozen bangdas. $\frac{1}{4}$ coconut. 6 green chillies. 4

DELIGHTS FROM MAHARASHTRA

flakes garlic. 1 lime-sized ball of tamarind. 4 flakes garlic, sliced finely. Handful of corriander leaves. ½ tsp. turmeric powder. 1 tsp. each of ground cumin seeds and corriander powder. Salt and chilli powder to taste

Cut the fishes after cleaning them into small pieces and apply on them salt, chilli and turmeric powder. Soak tamarind in 2 cups water for 5 minutes and then squeeze out the juice. Grind coconut, chillies and 4 flakes garlic to a paste. Heat 4 tblsps. oil and fry the sliced garlic to a red colour. Add fish and fry a little, add ground paste and spices, mix well and then put in the tamarind water. Cook till done. Serve decorated with sliced corriander leaves.

Prawn curry

500 gram prawns, cleaned and deviened. 1 tsp. turmeric powder. ½ coconut. 1 tsp. corriander seeds. 6 red chillies. 1 small onion. ½ cup tamarind water. Handful of corriander leaves. 2 medium onions, minced. 1 tsp. ground cumin seeds. Salt and chilli powder to taste.

Apply salt and turmeric on prawns and set aside for half an hour. Grind coconut, small onion, corriander seeds and chillies to a paste. Heat 4 tblsps. oil and fry onions to a pale gold colour. Add prawns and fry till they turn dry. Put in 1 cup water and tamarind water and cook till the prawns are almost done, then put in the coconut paste and powdered cumin seeds and continue cooking till the prawns are done. Serve decorated with corriander leaves.

Prawn fry

1 kilo prawns, cleaned and deveined. 3 large onions, minced. ¼ coconut, grated finely. 4 flakes garlic sliced. 1 tsp. turmeric powder. Handful of corriander leaves. Salt and chilli powder to taste.

Apply salt and turmeric on prawns and set aside half an hour. Heat 6 tblsps. oil and put in the onions and fry till soft. Mix in the rest of the above ingredients. Cover tightly and sprinkle cold water on the lid. Let the prawns cook in their own juice till tender, then keep on stirring them till they turn brown. Serve hot garnished with sliced corriander leaves.

Prawn masala fry

500 grams prawns, shelled and deveined. ½ dry coconut. 5 red chillies. 1 tsp. fenugreek seeds. ½ tsp. mustard seeds. 1 tsp. turmeric powder. Handful of corriander leaves. Salt and lime juice to taste.

Apply salt and turmeric to prawns and set aside for half an hour. Fry coconut and fenugreek seeds to a red colour in a little oil and grind to a fine paste with chillies. Heat 8 tblsps. oil and toss in mustard, when the seeds stop popping, put in the prawns and fry till crisp and golden. Mix in the coconut paste and remove from fire. Sprinkle on top lime juice and corriander leaves before serving. You can preserve this dish for a few days.

Prawn bhajee sukha

500 grams small prawns, shelled and deveined. 4 medium onions, minced. 2 medium potatoes, peeled and cubed. 4 green chillies, minced. 1-inch piece ginger, minced. 6 flakes garlic, crushed. 1 tsp. cumin seeds. A few peppercorns. ½ tsp. turmeric powder. 1 tsp. garam masala. Handful of sliced corriander leaves. Salt and chilli powder to taste.

Apply salt and turmeric on prawns and set aside for half an hour. Heat 4 tblsps. oil and fry the onions lightly. Put in the prawns and cook till dry. Put in the rest of the above ingredients along with powdered cumin seeds and peppercorns. Cover tightly, sprinkle cold water over the lid and cook over a slow fire till both the prawns and potatoes are done. Serve decorated with 1 tblsp. grated coconut and a handful of corriander leaves.

Prawn and vegetable curry

500 grams prawns, shelled and deveined. 2 medium onions, minced. 2 medium potatoes, peeled and cubed. 100 grams shelled green peas. 1 small brinjal, diced. 1 drumstick, scraped and cut into 1-inch pieces. 2 medium tomatoes, blanched and sliced. 2 cocums. 4 green chillies. 1 small bunch corriander leaves. 1 small piece coconut. 5 flakes garlic. 1-inch piece ginger. 1 tsp. each of garam masala and turmeric powder. 1 tsp. ground cumin seeds. Salt and chilli powder to taste.

Grind chillies, corriander leaves, coconut, garlic and ginger to a paste. Apply salt and turmeric on prawns and set aside for half an hour. Clean and wash the cocums. Heat 5 tblsps. oil and fry the onions till soft. Add prawns and fry till dry. Mix in the vegetables with the exception of tomatoes, salt and spices and ground coconut paste. Fry for 5 minutes, then pour in 3 cups water. Cook till the prawns and the vegetables are almost done, then put in the tomatoes and cocums. When the vegetables and prawns are done, remove from fire. Garnish with corriander leaves and serve with plain boiled rice.

Prawn and peas mix

500 grams small prawns shelled and deviened. 500 grams shelled green peas. 250 grams onions, minced. 2 tblsps. grated coconut. Handful of corriander leaves. 8 flakes garlic. 1 big piece ginger. 8 green chillies. 1 tblsp. corriander powder. ½ tsp. turmeric powder. 1 tsp. ground cumin seeds. ½ cup tamarind water. Salt, jaggery and chilli powder to suit the taste.

Apply salt and turmeric on the prawns and set aside for half an hour. Grind ginger, garlic and chillies and mix with the prawns. Heat 5 tblsps. oil and add prawns and onions and fry till the mixture turns a rich red colour. Add all the spices and salt and 1 cup water and cook till the prawns are almost done. Put in the tamarind water, jaggery and peas and continue cooking till both the prawns and the peas are done. Serve garnished with coconut and corriander leaves.

DELIGHTS FROM MAHARASHTRA

Prawn and pumpkin curry

500 grams prawns, shelled and deveined. 500 grams pumpkin or marrow peeled and diced. 6 red chillies. 1 tsp. fenugreek seeds. 1 tblsp. corriander seeds. 1 medium onion. 1 small onion, finely sliced. A few curry leaves. 3 flakes garlic. 1 tsp. turmeric powder. 1 tsp. ground cumin seeds. ½ coconut. 1 lime-sized ball of tamarind. Salt to taste.

Fry all the spices, coconut, whole onion and garlic to a red colour and grind to a paste. Cover tamarind with ½ cup water for 5 minutes and then squeeze out the juice. Heat 5 tblsps. oil and fry the prawns till dry. Put in the pumpkin and 2 cups water and salt and cook till the prawns are almost done. Put in the tamarind and coconut paste and continue cooking till the prawns are done. Remove from fire and set aside. Heat 1 tblsp. oil and fry sliced onion and curry leaves nicely and put into the curry. Serve with boiled rice.

Fried prawns

1 kilo large prawns. 10 flakes garlic. 8 green chillies. 1 small piece coconut. 4 tblsps. thick tamarind juice. 1 tsp. turmeric powder. 1 tsp. garam masala. 1 tsp. ground cumin seeds. Salt and chilli powder to taste.

Clean and devein prawns. Make a slit on the back of each prawn halfway through and set aside. Grind all the above ingredients to a smooth paste and stuff into each prawn. Heat

6 tblsps. ghee and put in the prawns and fry to a golden colour on slow fire. Serve decorated with corriander leaves.

Masalayachi anda

4 eggs, hardboiled and shelled. 100 grams onions, sliced finely. ¼ coconut. 3 red chillies. 3 cloves. ½-inch piece cinnamon stick. 2 flakes garlic. Handful of corriander leaves. ½ tsp. turmeric powder. Salt to taste. ½ cup tamarind water.

Grind coconut, chillies and all the spices to a paste. Make fine slits on eggs and apply the paste nicely on them. Heat 4 tblsps. oil and fry the onions till soft, add eggs and fry for 5 minutes. Put in the tamarind water and cook till the gravy turns thick. Serve hot decorated with corriander leaves.

Eggs and potato curry

4 hard-boiled eggs, shelled. 250 grams potatoes, peeled and sliced. 100 grams onions, minced. 3 cups thin and 1 cup thick coconut milk. ½ tsp. turmeric powder. 1-inch piece ginger, minced. 4 flakes garlic, minced. 4 green chillies, slitted. A few curry leaves. ¼ tsp. fenugreek seeds. 1 tsp. garam masala. Handful of corriander leaves. Salt and chilli powder to taste.

Heat 2 tblsps. oil and toss in the fenugreek seeds, when they turn red, put in onions, garlic and ginger and fry till soft. Add all the spices, potatoes and salt and fry for 5 minutes. Put in the thin coconut milk and curry leaves and cook till the potatoes are tender, add thick coconut milk and halved eggs and simmer gently for 5 minutes. Remove from fire and sprinkle corriander leaves and if you like lime juice on the top.

Especial egg curry

4 eggs. 150 grams shelled peas. 5 flakes garlic. 2 medium onions, minced. 1 piece ginger, minced. 1 tsp. garam masala. ½ tsp. turmeric powder. 2 medium potatoes, peeled and sliced. 2 large tomatoes, blanched and sliced. Handful of corriander leaves. 4 green chillies, minced. 3 cups thin and 1 cup thick coconut milk. Salt and chilli powder to suit the taste.

Heat 4 tblsps. oil and fry onions, ginger, garlic and chillies to a light golden colour. Add all the spices, salt and tomatoes and cook till the tomatoes turn soft. Put in peas and potatoes, mix well then pour in thin coconut milk. When the vegetables turn soft, pour in the thick coconut milk, bring slowly to a boil, then break one egg at a time into the boiling curry after an interval of half a minute, putting each slightly away from the other. Remove the curry after boiling the eggs in it for 5 minutes. Serve hot garnished with corriander leaves.

MUTTON & CHICKEN

2 big onions. 1 small piece dry coconut. 4 cardamoms. ½ tsp. each of anise and corriander seeds. 6 flakes garlic. 4 green chillies. 1 piece ginger. 1 tsp. turmeric powder. 3 cups thin and 1 cup thick coconut milk. Salt and chilli powder to taste. Handful of corriander leaves.

Grind chillies, garlic and ginger to a paste. Mix with turmeric and salt and apply on the mutton. Roast onions, coconut, cardamoms, anise and corriander seeds and grind to a paste. Heat 5 tblsps. oil and fry mutton to a red colour. Add thin coconut milk and cook till the mutton is almost done. Pour in the thick coconut milk, potatoes and ground coconut paste and continue cooking till the mutton is tender and gravy quite thick. Serve decorated with corriander leaves.

Mutton chaps masaledar

1 kilo mutton chaps. 250 grams beaten curds. 10 flakes garlic. 8 green chillies. 2-inch piece ginger. 2 tsps. garam masala. ¼ coconut. 1 tsp. turmeric powder. 1 medium onion. 100 grams each of baby onions and baby potatoes boiled and peeled. Salt and chilli powder to taste.

Grind big onion, coconut, ginger, garlic and chillies to a paste and mix into the curds along with salt and all the powdered spices. Put in the chaps and set aside for 1 hour, or so. Heat 5 tblsps. ghee and fry the chaps to a rich golden colour. Cover with hot water and cook till the chaps are almost done, put in the lightly fried whole onions and potatoes and continue cooking till the chaps are done and the gravy is thick. Serve decorated with corriander leaves.

Spicy mutton

500 grams mutton. 10 flakes garlic. 6 green chillies. 1-inch piece ginger. 1 tsp. turmeric powder. 2 large onions. ½ coconut. 4 cloves. 6 peppercorns. 1-inch piece cinnamon stick. 1 tblsp. corriander seeds. 3 big tomatoes, peeled and sliced. 1 tblsp. poppy seeds. Salt and chilli powder to taste.

Fry coconut, poppy seeds and all the whole spices to a red colour in ghee and grind to a paste. Grind separately garlic, ginger and chillies. Mix in salt and turmeric and rub on the mutton and set aside for half an hour. Heat 4 tblsps. ghee and fry the onions to a golden colour. Put in the mutton and tomatoes. Mix well. Cover tightly and sprinkle cold water over the lid. Cook the mutton without adding water over a slow fire till it is tender. Mix in the ground coconut paste and half cup hot water. Continue cooking till the gravy turns thick. Serve decorated with corriander leaves.

Mutton curry No. 1

500 grams mutton, cut into serving portions. 3 medium onions, finely sliced. 4-inch piece ginger. 10 flakes garlic. 3 red chillies. 1 tsp. turmeric powder. ½ dry coconut. 1 large onion. 1-inch piece cinnamon stick. 1 tblsp. poppy seeds. 4 cardamoms. 4 cloves. 8 pepper corns. Salt and chilli powder to taste.

Grind ginger, garlic and chillies. Mix with salt and turmeric and apply on the mutton and set aside for 1 hour. Roast copra and 1 big onion on fire till red and then grind to a paste along with poppy seeds and whole spices. Heat 5 tblsps. ghee and fry onions till brown. Cover with hot water and cook till almost done. Mix in the coconut paste and continue cooking till tender and the gravy turns quite thick. Serve garnished with corriander leaves.

Mutton curry No. 2

500 grams mutton, cut into serving portions. 3 cups thin and 1 cup thick coconut milk. 1 small ball of tamarind. 4 medium onions, finely sliced. 1 tsp. turmeric powder. 8 flakes garlic. 1-inch piece ginger 2 tblsps. finely grated coconut. 4 red chillies. 1 tblsp. garam masala. 1 tblsp. each of cumin, corriander and poppy seeds. ¼ tsp. saffron or essence of saffron. Salt to taste.

If you are using saffron strands, soak it in 1 tsp. hot water for 5 minutes and then crush to a paste. Cover tamarind with water for 5 minutes then squeeze out the juice. Grind grated coconut, chillies, cumin, corriander and poppy seeds to a paste. Grind ginger and garlic to a paste. Mix in salt and turmeric and rub on the mutton. Set aside for 1 hour. Heat 5 tblsps. ghee and fry sliced onions to a golden colour. Add coconut paste and fry till the ghee floats to the top. Add mutton and fry to a rich red colour. Put in the thin coconut milk and garam masala and cook till the mutton is tender. Pour in the tamarind water and thick coconut milk and continue cooking until a thick and creamy gravy is left. Serve decorated with corriander leaves.

Mutton kofta curry

3 medium onions. 1-inch piece ginger. 4 flakes garlic. 6 green chillies. 1 tblsp. each of poppy seeds and sesame seeds. 25 grams each of cashewnuts and roasted groundnuts. 1 small piece coconut. 4 cups coconut milk. 1 small ball of tamarind. Salt and chilli powder to taste. 1 tsp. each of garam masala and turmeric powder. Handful of sliced corriander leaves.

For koftas......500 grams minced mutton. 4 flakes garlic. 1-inch piece ginger. 2 green chillies. A big handful of corriander leaves. 1 tsp. garam masala. 1 tblsp. each of poppy seeds and sesame seeds. Salt to taste. 1 egg.

Grind together all the kofta ingredients with the exception of egg to a smooth paste. Mix in the egg, knead to a smooth mixture, then form into small balls or koftas and deep fry to a golden brown colour. Cover tamarind with half cup water for 5 minutes and squeeze out the juice. Grind ginger, garlic, onions, chillies, nuts, poppy and sesame seeds and coconut to a paste. Heat 5 tblsps. ghee and fry the paste to a rich golden colour. Add the ground spices, turmeric and salt. Mix well and pour in the coconut milk and tamarind. Cook over a slow fire till the gravy turns a little thick, then put in the koftas and simmer gently for another 5 minutes. Serve hot garnished with corriander leaves.

Poha kheema

250 grams kheema or minced mutton. 250 grams poha. 2 big onions, minced. 1-inch piece ginger, minced. 4 flakes garlic, minced. 5 green chillies. 2 tblsps. grated coconut. Handful of corriander leaves. ½ tsp. turmeric powder. 1 tsp. garam masala. Salt, lime juice and chilli powder to taste.

Clean and wash poha in water nicely and squeeze out the water. Heat 4 tblsps. oil and fry onions, ginger, garlic and chillies till soft. Put in the kheema and ground spices and salt and fry till it turns dry and crumbly. Cover with hot water and cook till the kheema is almost done. Put in the poha, mix well and continue cooking till the kheema is cooked and dry. Serve hot garnished with coconut and corriander leaves and sprinkled with lime juice.

Kheema brinjal mix

500 grams large brinjals. 250 grams kheema. 2 big onions, minced. 4 green chillies, minced. 4 flakes garlic, minced. 1-inch piece ginger, minced. ½ tsp. turmeric powder. 1 tsp. garam masala. 125 grams beaten curds. 1 cup coconut milk. 2 tblsps. grated coconut. Handful of sliced corriander leaves.

Hold brinjals on gas or charcoal flame and roast turning frequently till the skin turns black and wrinkled. Toss into cold water. Peel nicely and mash the brinjals to a pulp. Heat 4 tblsps. oil and fry onions, ginger, garlic and chillies till soft.

Put in the kheema, salt and ground spices and cook till dry and crumbly. Put in dahi. Cover tightly, sprinkle cold water on the lid and cook over a slow fire without adding water till the kheema is cooked. Mix in the coconut milk and brinjal pulp and continue cooking till the mixture turns thick. Serve hot garnished with coconut and corriander leaves.

Kheema

500 grams kheema or minced meat. 250 grams onions, finely sliced. 1-inch piece ginger, minced. 4 flakes garlic, minced. 4 green chillies, minced. 1 tsp. garam masala. ½ tsp. turmeric powder. 2 cups coconut milk. 25 grams blanched and sliced almonds. 2 tblsps. each of fried raisins and charoli. 2 tblsps. grated coconut. ¼ tsp. ground anise seeds. 1 tblsp. poppy seeds, ground, ¼ tsp. saffron strands or essence of saffron. Salt, chilli powder and lime juice to suit the taste.

Heat 5 tblsps. ghee and fry onions, ginger, garlic and chillies till soft. Mix in all the spices and poppy seeds and fry briefly. Put in the kheema and fry till dry and crumbly. Pour in coconut milk and add salt. Cover tightly and cook on a slow fire till the kheema is tender and dry. Mix in fried nuts and raisins, corriander leaves and saffron essence and remove from fire. If you are using saffron strands soak in 1 tblsp. hot water for 5 minutes and crush to a paste before putting into the kheema. Serve hot garnished with coconut and almonds.

Kheema-Stuffed cauliflower

1 medium cauliflower. 250 grams kheema. 1 tblsp. poppy seeds. 25 grams each of cashewnuts and roasted groundnuts. 2 large onions. 1-inch piece ginger. 8 flakes garlic. 4 medium tomatoes, blanched and pureed. 1 tsp. each of garam masala and turmeric powder. 1 cup coconut milk. Handful of sliced corriander leaves. A few blanched and sliced and fried almonds. Salt and chilli powder to suit the taste.

Grind onion, ginger and garlic to a paste. Heat 4 tblsps. ghee and fry half of the ground paste to a brown colour. Put in garam masala and half of turmeric powder. Fry briefly, then put in the kheema and salt. Fry till kheema turns dry and crumbly. Cover with hot water and cook till it turns tender and completely dry. Remove from fire and grind to a paste along with cashewnuts, groundnuts and poppy seeds. Wash the cauliflower nicely and cut the stalk very close. Hold the vegetable against light to check for any blemish. Then stuff the kheema mixture carefully between the flowerets. Heat 5 tblsps. oil and fry the remaining onion paste to a golden colour. Put in turmeric, tomatoes, salt and chilli powder and cook till soft. Mix in the coconut milk, then put in the cauliflower with the head downwards. Cook covered on a slow fire till the cauliflower is done. Serve garnished with sliced almonds and corriander leaves.

Kheema-stuffed bittergourds

500 grams bittergourds of uniform size. 2 big

onions. 5 flakes garlic. 125 grams beaten curds. 1 tsp. turmeric powder. ¼ tsp. grated jaiphal. A big pinch mace. 1 tsp. garam masala. Handful of corriander leaves.

For filling......250 grams minced meat. 1 big onion. 5 flakes garlic. A big piece ginger. 1 small piece coconut. 1 tsp. poppy seeds. 1 tsp. garam masala. Salt and chilli powderto taste.

Mix 1 cup hot water with curds and beat nicely. Grind onion, ginger, garlic, coconut and poppy seeds to a paste. Heat 4 tblsps. oil and fry the onion paste to a golden colour. Put in the ground spices and kheema and salt and fry till dry and crumbly. Cover with hot water and cook till the kheema turns tender and dry. Peel bitergourds and make a deep slit in the centre of each. Sprinkle nicely with salt and set aside for 5 hours. Drain out the water and wash in several changes of water, squeeze dry after each washing. Bring a dekchi of water to a boil, toss in the gourds and boil for 1 minute. Drain out the water and set aside. The above procedure removes the bitterness of the gourds. Remove the inner pith of the gourds and fill nicely with kheema, then tie each karela with thread to keep stuffing intact. Grind onion and garlic to a paste. Heat 4 tblsps. of oil and fry the ground paste to a rich golden colour. Put in garam masala, turmeric, mace and jaiphal and fry briefly. Put in the gourds and then put curds over top. Cover tightly and cook over a slow fire till the gourds are tender and dry. Serve hot garnished with corriander leaves.

Kheema-stuffed parval

300 grams parval. Prepare kheema filling in the same way as shown in the above recipe. 1 cup gram flour. 1 big cup bread crumbs. A pinch soda bicarbonate. Salt and chilli powder to taste.

Fry gram flour in a little oil to a light brown colour. Mix in soda salt and chilli powder along with enough water to form a thick batter. Wash and steam parval till done. Cut into 2-inch pieces, remove inner seeds, then stuff the pieces of parval nicely with kheema. Dip in batter, roll lightly in crumbs and deep fry to a golden brown colour. Drain and serve piping hot accompanied with chutney of your choice.

Brain masaledar

2 sheeps brains, boiled......see helpful hints. 2 big onions, minced. 8 flakes garlic. 1-inch piece ginger. 6 green chillies. 1 tsp. each of garam masala and corriander powder. 2 tblsps grated coconut. Handful of sliced corriander leaves. 2 medium tomatoes, peeled and sliced. $\frac{1}{2}$ tsp. turmeric powder. Salt and chilli powder to taste.

Grind ginger, garlic and chillies to a paste and apply nicely on the brains. Heat 4 tblsps. oil and fry onions to a rich golden colour. Add salt and ground spices, fry briefly, put in the brains and fry them nicely. Put in tomatoes and coconut and cook till the gravy turns thick. Serve garnished with corriander leaves.

Brain curry

2 sheeps brains, boiled......see helpful hints. 8

flakes garlic. 1-inch piece ginger. 1 tsp. garam masala. ½ tsp. turmeric powder. 6 green chillies. 2 medium onions, minced. 1 cup coconut milk. Salt and chilli powder to taste. Handful of corriander leaves.

Grind ginger, garlic and chillies and apply on the brains. Heat 4 tblsps. oil and fry the onions to a rich brown colour. Mix in all the ground spices and salt. Put in the brains and fry nicely. Pour in the coconut milk and cook till the gravy turns a little thick. Serve hot garnished with corriander leaves.

Spicy liver

1 liver, cut into small pieces. 1 small piece dry coconut. 4 green chillies. Handful of corriander leaves. 6 flakes garlic. 2 large onions, minced. 4 medium tomatoes, peeled and sliced. 1 tsp. each of garam masala and corriander powder. ½ tsp turmeric powder. Salt and chilli powder to taste.

Grind to a paste coconut, chillies and garlic. Heat 4 tblsps. oil and fry onions to a brown colour. Add the ground paste and fry till the oil floats to the top. Add all the spices, salt and liver and cook till dry. Put in the tomatoes, cover tightly and cook without adding water till the liver is tender. Serve garnished with corriander leaves.

Liver kababs

1 liver, cut into cubes. 50 grams beaten curds. 1 tblsp. garam masala. 4 flakes garlic. 1-inch piece ginger. 4 green chillies. A big pinch each of nutmeg and mace. Salt and chilli powder to taste.

DELIGHTS FROM MAHARASHTRA

Grind garlic, ginger and chillies to a paste. Mix into the curds along with salt and all the spices. Put liver into curds and set aside 1 hour. Put liver on skewers and stand for 10 minutes, pour little ghee or oil over liver and roast or grill the liver till a rich red colour.

Chicken and peas curry

1 chicken, disjointed. 250 grams green peas, shelled. 125 grams onions finely sliced. 8 flakes garlic. 2-inch piece ginger. 8 green chillies. 1 tblsp. garam masala. 1 tblsp. corriander powder. A big pinch each of grated nutmeg and mace. Handful of corriander leaves. 1 tsp. turmeric powder. 250 grams beaten curds. 3 cups thin and 1 cup thick coconut milk. 25 grams cashewnuts. Salt and chilli powder to taste.

Grind ginger, garlic and chillies to a paste. Mix the paste into curds along with all the spices and salt and chicken and set aside. Heat 6 tblsps. ghee and fry the onions to a red colour. Put in the chicken. Cover tightly and cook till the chicken turns dry. Then fry it till it turns red. Add cashewnuts and pour in the thin coconut milk and cook over a slow fire till the chicken turns almost tender. Then add peas and thick coconut milk and continue cooking till the chicken turns tender. Serve decorated with corriander leaves.

Chicken curry

1 chicken, disjointed. 3 cups thin and 1 cup thick coconut milk. 4 green and 4 red chillies. 1 tblsp. garam masala. 25 grams cashewnuts. 25 grams

roasted groundnuts. 25 grams each of fried cashewnuts and raisins. 1 tsp. turmeric powder. 3 medium onions. 5 flakes garlic. 1-inch piece ginger. A big pinch each of nutmeg and mace. Handful of corriander leaves. Salt and chilli powder to taste. Grind ginger, garlic, chillies, cashewnuts and groundnuts to a paste. Roast 1 onion on fire till black. Peel and grind to a paste. Heat 6 tblsps. ghee and fry the minced onions and ground garlic and onion paste to a rich red colour. Add all the spices and salt, then put in the chicken and fry to a red colour. Pour in the thin coconut milk and cook till it turns tender. Add thick milk, mix well, bring to a boil and remove from fire. Serve garnished with fried raisins, cashewnuts and corriander leaves.

RICE RECIPES

Mutton pullao

2 cups Delhi rice. 4 red chillies. 3 green chillies. ¼ small bunch corriander leaves. 500 grams mutton, cut into serving portions. 4 cloves. 4 cardamoms. 1 tsp. corriander seeds. 1-inch piece cinnamon stick. 1-inch piece ginger, minced. 3 big onions, minced. 1 small onion, cut into thin rings. 6 flakes garlic. ¼ coconut. 4 big tomatoes blanched and sliced. 25 grams each of fried cashewnuts and raisins. 1 tsp. turmeric powder. Salt to suit the taste.

Wash and soak the rice in 4 cups of water for 2 hours. Fry onion rings in oil till crisp and golden and set aside. Grind all the spices, coconut, chillies, ginger and garlic to a paste. Heat 6 tblsps. oil and fry the minced onion to a golden colour. Put in the ground paste and continue cooking till the paste turns golden and a nice aroma comes out of it. Put in the mutton and tomatoes and cook till dry. Cover with hot water and cook till the mutton turns tender and dry. Put in the rice and turmeric and the water in which the rice was soaked, bring to a boil, reduce heat to simmering and cook till the rice turns tender and completely dry. Serve garnished with cashewnuts, onion rings and raisins.

Prawn pullao

250 grams rice of good quality. 250 grams prawns, shelled and deviened. 3 green and 3 red chillies. 1 tblsp. corriander seeds. 1-inch piece cinnamon stick. 4 cloves. 4 cardamoms. A big handful each of corriander and mint leaves. 1 tsp. saffron strands or essence of saffron. ½ cup curds.

15 cashewnuts. 2 big onions. Salt to taste. ½-inch piece ginger. 5 flakes garlic.

Grind chillies, corriander seeds, mint, corriander leaves, ginger, garlic and cashewnuts to a paste and mix into the curds along with salt. If you are using saffron strands then soak in 2 tblsps hot milk for 5 minutes, then crush to a paste. Put prawns in the curd mixture and set aside for half an hour. Heat 4 tblsps. oil and put in the prawn mixture. Cover tightly and cook without adding water till the prawns are done. Remove from fire and set aside. Heat 4 tblsps. oil in a separate vessel and fry the onion rings to a golden colour. Remove and set aside. Put a little more oil into the vessel and put in the whole spices, then add rice and salt. Mix well and then pour in 500 grams water. Bring to a boil, reduce heat and cook till the rice is almost tender and dry. Remove from fire and keep aside. Grease a vessel nicely and then arrange in it layers of rice, prawns and fried onions. Keep some onions aside for garnishing. Start and finish with a layer of rice. Sprinkle saffron on top. Cover tightly and cook over a very slow fire for 10 minutes. Serve garnished with remaining onions and corriander leaves.

Kheema pullao

250 grams Delhi rice. 250 grams minced meat. 2 tblsps. finely grated coconut. 1-inch piece cinnamon stick, broken into bits. 4 cloves. 2 big and 2 small cardamoms, peeled. 1 bay leaf, crumpled. 2 tsps. corriander powder. 1 tsp. garam masala.

3 red chillies, broken into bits. 2 medium onions, cut into thin rings. A handful of mint leaves. 1 tsp. turmeric powder. ½ cup beaten curds. 5 flakes garlic. A big piece ginger. Salt to taste. 2 hard-boiled eggs, cut into quarters. Handful of corriander leaves.

Fry the onions in ghee till golden, mix in the mint, stir for a minute and remove from fire. Heat 4 tblsps. ghee and put in the whole spices, add kheema, ground spices and salt and ginger and garlic and red chillies and cook till the kheema turns dry. Put in 1 cup hot water and cook till tender and completely dry. Add cleaned and washed rice, mix well and then pour in enough water to stand 1-inch above the level of the rice. Bring to a boil, reduce heat and cook till the rice is almost tender and dry. Mix in the curds, coconut and onion mixture. Cover once again and continue cooking over a very slow fire till the rice is done. Serve hot garnished with boiled eggs and corriander leaves.

Valchi khichdi

250 grams Delhi rice. 250 grams val or sprouted field beans. (Whole) 4 flakes garlic. 4 green chillies. 1-inch piece ginger. 1 small onion. 1 small piece coconut. 2 medium onions. ¼ coconut, grated. 2 tblsps. beaten curds. ½ tsp. turmeric powder. 4 cloves. 2 cardamoms. 1-inch piece cinnamon stick. 25 grams each of fried groundnuts and cashewnuts. Salt to taste. 1 tsp. ground cumin seeds. 1 tblsp. corriander seeds.

Pound together corriander seeds, cloves, cardamoms and cinnamon. Mix together curds and grated coconut. Grind together ginger, chillies and garlic. Fry small onion and the piece of coconut to a red colour and grind to a paste with a little water. Heat 4 tblsps. oil and put in all the spices and onions, ground garlic paste. Fry till soft and then add beans, washed and cleaned rice, salt and fried onion paste. Mix well, then pour in enough water to stand 1-inch above the level of the rice. Bring to a boil, reduce heat and cook till the rice is almost tender and dry. Then mix in curd mixture and continue cooking over a very slow fire till the rice is done. Serve hot garnished with nuts.

Kesari bhat

2 cups of rice. 4½ cups milk. ½ tsp. saffron strands. 1 cup sugar. 25 grams each of almonds and pistachios and raisins. 1 ripe mango, peeled and sliced. 2 rings canned pineapple, cubed. 1 sweet apple, sliced. 1 tblsp. cardamom seeds, coarsely powdered.

Fry the nuts and raisins. Soak saffron in 1 tblsp. hot milk for 5 minutes, then crush to a paste. Heat 4 tblsps. ghee, put in cardamoms and then rice. Mix well and put in the milk. Bring to a boil, reduce heat and cook till the rice is almost done. Put in the sugar and the fruits. Cover tightly and cook over a very slow fire till the rice is done. Mix in the saffron and remove from fire. Serve garnished with nuts and raisins.

DELIGHTS FROM MAHARASHTRA

Mitha bhat

2 cups rice. 3 cups thin and 1 cup thick coconut milk. 1 cup finely grated jaggery. 25 grams each of fried almonds, raisins and pistachios. 1 tsp. cardamom seeds. $\frac{1}{2}$ tsp. saffron strands.

Soak saffron in 1 tblsp. hot milk for 5 minutes and then crush to a paste. Heat 4 tblsps. ghee and put in the rice and cardamom seeds and thin coconut milk. Bring to a boil, reduce heat and cook till the moisture is almost absorbed, then pour in the thick milk. Continue cooking till the rice is almost done, then mix in the jaggery. Now cook over a very slow fire till the rice is done. Mix in the saffron and remove from fire. Serve garnished with nuts and raisins.

Tomato bhat

450 grams rice. 1 kilo tomatoes, peeled, depiped and pureed. 2 big onions, cut into thin rings. 4 flakes garlic. 1-inch piece ginger. A few peppercorns. 4 cloves. 1-inch piece cinnamon stick, broken into bits. 2 cardamoms, peeled. $\frac{1}{2}$ tsp. turmeric powder. 2 tblsps, grated coconut. Handful of sliced corriander leaves. Salt to suit the taste.

Mix 1 litre water in tomato juice and strain. Grind ginger and garlic to a paste. Heat 4 tblsps. ghee and put in the whole spices and then garlic, ginger and onions and fry till brown. Add turmeric, salt and rice. Mix well and then put in the tomato juice. Bring to a boil reduce heat and cook till the rice is done. Serve garnished with coconut and corriander leaves.

Mango bhat

450 grams rice. 1 kilo pureed sweet mangoes. 25 grams each of fried cashewnuts, almonds, pistachios and raisins. A few drops either essence of rose or kewda. Silver foil.

Mix 1 kilo water with pureed mangoes. Heat 3 tblsps. ghee and put in the rice, fry a little and then pour in the mango juice, bring to a boil, reduce heat and cook till the rice is done. Mix in essence, nuts and raisins and remove from fire. Serve decorated with foil.

Dal bhat

250 grams Delhi rice. 2 tblsps. each of toovar, moong, urad, masoor and channa dal. 2 medium onions, cut into thin rings. $\frac{1}{4}$ litre milk. 1 tsp. turmeric powder. 1-inch piece ginger. A few peppercorns. 4 cloves. 2 peeled cardamoms. 1-inch piece cinnamon stick, broken into bits. 1 bay leaf, crumpled. Salt to suit the taste.

Pound the whole spices coarsely. Mince together ginger and one onion. Fry the remaining onion till crisp and golden and set aside. Half boil both the rice and the dals separately. Strain the water and set aside. Heat 4 tblsps. ghee and put in the spices, ginger and minced onion and fry till soft. Add salt, turmeric, rice and dals. Mix well and then put in the milk. Cover tightly and cook over a slow fire till the rice and the dals are done. Remove from fire and serve garnished with fried onion rings.

Masala bhat

250 grams Delhi rice. 50 grams tindlis. 100 grams green peas. 1 medium brinjal. 2 medium potatoes. 50 grams raw groundnuts. 25 grams cashewnuts. 4 green chillies. A few peppercorns. $\frac{1}{2}$-inch piece cinnamon stick. 4 cloves. A few curry leaves. 1 tblsp. corriander seeds. 1 tblsp. cumin seeds. 1 tsp. sesame seeds. $\frac{1}{2}$ tsp. mustard seeds. A pinch asafoetida. 1 small piece dry coconut. 4 tblsps. grated fresh coconut. Handful of finely sliced corriander leaves. Salt to suit the taste. $\frac{1}{2}$ tsp. turmeric powder.

Soak groundnuts in water for 15 minutes, then drain out the water and remove the peels. Roast together peppercorns, cloves, dry coconut, cinnamon, corriander, sesame and half of the cumin seeds and powder the mixture. Wash and cut the tindlis lengthwise. Shell the peas. Cut the brinjal and potatoes into cubes. Heat 4 tblsps. ghee and put in asafoetida, mustard and the remaining cumin seeds. When the seeds stop popping, add the curry leaves, chillies and all the vegetables fry for 5 minutes. Put in the rice, turmeric and salt. Mix well and then put in the powdered spices, cashewnuts and peanuts, then put in enough water to stand 1-inch above the level of the rice. Bring to a boil, reduce heat and cook till the rice turns tender and dry. Remove from fire, pour on top 2 tblsps ghee and serve garnished with grated coconut and corriander leaves.

Potato bhat

2 cups Delhi rice. 250 grams potatoes, boiled and peeled. 1 tblsp. gram flour. 125 well-beaten curds. 125 grams ghee. 75 grams khoya. 2 cardamoms. 2 cloves. ½-inch piece cinnamon stick. 1 tsp. corriander powder. A big pinch of anise seeds. 1 tsp. cumin seeds. 2 medium onions, minced. 6 flakes garlic. 1-inch piece ginger. 1 tsp. garam masala. 1 small onion. 1 tsp. turmeric powder. 1 tblsp. rose water. 50 grams fried cashewnuts. Salt and chilli powder to taste.

Mix together potatoes, gram flour, salt, chilli powder and garam masala together. Grind half inch piece ginger, 2 flakes garlic and the small onion to a paste and mix with the potatoes. Knead the potatoes to a smooth paste and form into small balls. Deep fry the balls to a golden brown colour. Drain and set aside. Grind the remaining onions, ginger and garlic to a paste. Heat half of ghee and fry the onion paste till red. Add the curds and cook till smooth. Add potato balls. Mix and sprinkle on top 4 tblsps. milk. Cook over a slow fire till almost all the moisture is absorbed. Heat the remaining ghee and put in the whole spices and rice. Add 4 cups water and salt and bring to a boil. Reduce heat to simmering and cook till the rice turns almost tender and dry. Take a greased flame-proof glass dish and arrange rice and potato mixture in layers in it and then cashewnuts and 25 grams of fried raisins. Cover very tightly and cook over a very gentle fire for 10 minutes, or till the rice turns completely tender and dry. Serve in the dish itself.

TEA-TIME SAVOURIES

Batata vada

1 cup gram flour. 4 medium potatoes, boiled and peeled. ½ tsp. turmeric powder. 4 flakes garlic. ½-inch piece ginger. 4 green chillies. Handful of corriander leaves. Pinch of soda. Salt and chilli powder to taste.

Blend together gram flour, salt, soda and turmeric powder. Add enough water to form a thick batter. Put in 1 tblsp. of hot melted oil and set aside for about half an hour. Grind ginger, garlic, chillies and corriander leaves to a paste. Cut potatoes finely with a knife and mix in the salt and the ground paste. Form into round balls, dip in the batter and deep fry a few at a time to a golden brown colour. Drain thoroughly and serve with sukhi chutney.

Kanda vada

2 bunches of spring onions or 2 medium onions. 4 flakes garlic. ½-inch piece ginger. Pinch of soda. 4 green chillies. Handful of corriander leaves. ½ tsp. turmeric powder. Salt and chilli powder to taste. Gram flour.

Crush together ginger and garlic to a paste. Finely slice the onions, chillies and corriander leaves. Mix together the sliced ingredients with ginger and garlic paste and all the spices, salt and soda, then add enough flour to the mixture to bind the ingredients together, do not add any water. Form into thin round vadas and deep fry a few at a time to a golden brown colour. Drain thoroughly and serve with chutney of your choice.

Alu vadi

6 tender arvi leaves. 1 lime-sized ball of tamarind. 125 grams cooked minced meat. 6 flakes garlic. 35 grams gram flour. 1 small bunch corriander leaves. 1-inch piece ginger. 4 cloves. ½-inch piece cinnamon stick. 3 green chillies. 3 red chillies. 3 small cardamoms. ½ tsp. corriander seeds. 1 tsp. cumin seeds. Salt to taste.

Soak tamarind in 4 tblsps. water for 5 minutes, then squeeze out the juice. Roast and grind all the spices to a paste. Put the spices in meat and grind along with ginger, garlic, chillies and corriander leaves to a very smooth paste. Mix together meat, gram flour and tamarind water to form a thick paste. Clean the leaves properly. Remove the hard veins with a sharp knife taking care not to tear the leaves. Place one arvi leaf on the table on the wrong side and spread a thin layer of paste on this, spread another leaf on this and repeat the process until you have used up all the paste and leaves. Turn in the edges on both the sides and roll tightly and neatly into a roll. Tie with thread and steam for half an hour, or until tender. Remove, cut off the string and cut into thin slices and then shallow fry in oil or ghee till golden coloured. Serve immediately.

Chakali

125 grams gram flour. 375 grams rice flour. 2 tblsps. til seeds. 1 tblsp. chilli powder. ¼ tsp. asafoetida. 2 tblsps. butter. Salt to suit the taste. 1 tblsp. turmeric powder.

DELIGHTS FROM MAHARASHTRA

Mix together all the dry ingredients. Rub in the butter, then put in enough water to make a soft and pliable dough. Heat enough peanut oil to smoking and take a small ball of the dough and put one by one into the chakali mould, hold it over the pan and press the lever. Fry the chakalis a few at a time till golden and crisp. Drain thoroughly, cool and store in airtight container. These chakalies can be preserved for a few days.

Bhel puri

4 cups puffed rice or kurmura. 1 cup each of chivda......see section on Gujerati cuisine and sev. 1 medium potato, boiled, peeled and diced. 1 small cucumber, peeled and sliced finely. 1 small onion, minced. 1 firm tomato, diced. 1 small raw mango, peeled and diced. 2 tblsps. finely grated coconut. $\frac{1}{4}$ small bunch of finely sliced corriander leaves. Strained juice of 1 lime. 1 tsp. garam masala. Salt to suit the taste.

Tikhi chutney......1 bunch corriander leaves. Handful mint leaves. 6 green chillies. 1-inch piece ginger. 6 flakes garlic. 8 peppercorns. $\frac{1}{2}$-inch piece cinnamon stick. 2 cardamoms. Salt to taste.

Mithi chutney......1 lime-sized ball of tamarind. 15 pitted and sliced dates. Salt to taste.

For puries...... 50 grams each of suji and maida. Salt to taste.

Grind all the ingredients of tikhi chutney to a very smooth paste with little water. Soak tamarind in $1\frac{1}{2}$ cups hot water for 5 minutes, then squeeze out the pulp. Grind dates to a **very** smooth paste and stir into tamarind water along with salt and chilli powder. Mix together rava, maida and salt, then add enough water to form a stiff dough. Set aside for 15 minutes, then roll the dough out as thinly as you can with the help of a little dry flour. Cut into tiny rounds not bigger then 50 naya paise coin and deep fry a few at a time till crisp and golden. Drain thoroughly, set aside 6 puries for garnishing and crush the rest coarsely. Combine together puffed rice, sev, chivda, cucumber, onion, tomato, mango and crushed puries. Mix in tikhi and mithi chutney and lime juice. Sprinkle on top coconut and corriander leaves and garnish with whole puries. Bhel is eaten with puries and not with a spoon. If you like you can omit the coconut and vegetables from the bhel.

Coconut kababs

500 grams potatoes, boiled, peeled and mashed. 2 cups grated coconut. 4 green chillies. 1-inch piece ginger. 2 small onions. A few curry leaves. 1 medium firm tomato, sliced into thin and small pieces. 2 eggs, beaten. 1 cup bread crumbs. $\frac{1}{4}$ tsp. turmeric powder. A big handful of corriander leaves. Salt to taste. $\frac{1}{2}$ tsp. roasted and pounded cumin seeds.

Grind coconut, ginger, chillies, onions and corriander and curry leaves coarsely without adding water. Add turmeric powder, tomato and cumin seeds. Knead the potatoes into smooth mixture, form into kababs around the coconut mixture, dip in eggs, roll in crumbs and deep fry to a golden brown colour. Drain and serve hot.

SWEETS & DESSERTS

Dal ladu

1 kilo channa dal. ½ kilo khoya. 1 kilo ground sugar. 1 tblsp. cardamom seeds. 25 grams each of finely sliced almonds, pistachios and melon seeds. Silver foil. 10 tblsps. ghee.

Soak the dal in water whole night. Next morning, drain out the water thoroughly and dry for a little while, then grind to a paste. Heat ghee and fry the dal to a golden colour. Put in the khoya and cook till it turns golden also and the mixture turns smooth. Add the rest of the ingredients, mix nicely and remove from fire. Cool till bearably hot and form into round ladus or balls. Cover with foil and set aside to turn cold and hard, then store in air-tight container.

Besan ladu

½ kilo each of besan and rava. 250 grams ghee. 1 kilo powdered sugar. 1 tblsp. cardamom seeds. 25 grams each of sliced almonds, pistachios and raisins. A few drops essence of saffron. ½ kilo khoya.

Fry both the flours separately in ghee to a nice golden colour, then mix both the flours together, and put in the khoya and fry till the khoya turns red and the mixture turns smooth. Mix in the rest of the above ingredients and remove from fire. Cool till bearably hot and form into round balls or ladus. Set aside to turn cold and hard and then store in airtight container.

Rava and coconut ladu

1 kilo rava. 1 coconut, finely grated. 1 kilo powdered sugar. ½ kilo khoya. 250 grams ghee. 1 tblsp. cardamom seeds. A few drops essence of saffron. 25 grams each of sliced almonds, pistachios and raisins. Silver foil.

Heat ghee and fry the coconut to a red colour. Remove the coconut from ghee and put rava in it and fry to a red colour, then put in the khoya and continue frying till it turns red and the mixture smooth. Mix in the rest of the above ingredients and remove from fire. Cool till bearably hot and form into round balls or ladus. Cover with foil, set aside to turn cold and hard and then store in airtight tin.

Rava ladu

500 grams rava. 100 grams ghee. 500 grams powdered sugar. 50 grams each of finely chopped raisins. 50 grams fried and finely sliced cashewnuts. 1 tblsp. cardamom seeds.

Heat ghee and fry the rava over a low fire till it turns light brown in colour. Mix in the rest of the above ingredients and remove from fire. Cool till bearably hot and then form into round ladus or balls. Set aside to turn cold and hard and then store in airtight tin.

Til ladu

1 kilo til seeds. 1 kilo chikki jaggery. ¼ kilo fried peanuts, coarsely pounded. ¼ dry coconut or copra, finely sliced. 125 grams roasted grams,

pounded coarsely. 25 grams sliced pistachios. 25 grams sliced raisins. 1 tblsp. cardamom seeds.

Pick and wash the til seeds and dry them in the sun. When still slightly damp, put then in a napkin and rub them so that the skin comes off. Melt jaggery and mix in all the above ingredients. When the mixture turns thick, remove from fire. Cool till bearably hot, grease or dust your hands with rice flour and form into small ladus not bigger than a small marble quickly otherwise the mixture will turn hard like toffee. When you have formed all the ladus set aside to turn cold and hard and then store in airtight container.

Boondi ladu

1 kilo gram flour. 1 kilo sugar. A few drops orange red food colouring. $\frac{1}{2}$ lime. $\frac{1}{2}$ cup milk. A few drops essence of saffron. 1 tblsp. cardamom seeds. $\frac{1}{4}$ tsp. salt. 2 tblsps. melted ghee. A pinch of baking powder.

Sieve together flour, baking powder and salt. Mix in ghee, milk and enough water to form a thick batter. Beat till the mixture turns very smooth, then mix in the colour and set aside for 15 minutes. Heat enough ghee for deep frying to smoking, lower the heat then take a sieve with large holes, hold it over the smoking fat and rub a little batter at a time through the sieve. Tap the sieve on inside edges of the pan to make the mixture fall through the holes into the hot ghee. Fry the boondi to a golden colour. Drain nicely cool and store in airtight container.

Put 250 grams water in sugar and prepare a thin syrup. Mix in the lime juice after straining it and set aside whole night. Next morning, place the syrup on fire and make a thick syrup of one-thread consistency. Mix in the essence and cardamom seeds, then take a little syrup at a time and mix in a little amount of boondi thoroughly and then form into ladus after greasing or dusting your hands with rice flour. After you have finished preparing one batch of ladus, prepare another, in this way go on making ladus till all the mixture has been used up. Set the ladus to turn hard and cold and then store in airtight container.

Shrikhandachi vadi

500 grams thick and slightly sour curds. 500 grams sugar. 50 grams each of almonds, pistachios and cashewnuts. A few drops essence of saffron. 1 tblsp. cardamom seeds.

Powder together pistachios and cardamoms. Slice almonds and cashewnuts finely. Tie the curds in a muslin cloth. Hang up from a hook or nail in the wall till all the water drips off from the curds. Remove the curds from the cloth and put in a heavy-bottomed vessel along with sugar and sliced nuts. Keep on stirring over a slow fire till the mixture turns thick and leaves the sides of the vessel. Add essence and remove from fire. Put in a greased thali and level the surface. Sprinkle on top pounded pistachios evenly and nicely. Set aside to turn cold and hard and then cut into any shape you like. Store in airtight tin.

Tilchi vadi

150 grams cleaned til or sesame seeds. 50 grams roasted peanuts or groundnuts. 1 tsp. cardamom seeds. $\frac{1}{4}$ cup powdered dry coconut. 250 grams sugar.

Roast sesame seeds over a tava to a light brown colour. When it cools a little grind to a powder with peanuts. Put 2 cups water in sugar and prepare a syrup of one-thread consistency. Put in the tils and cardamoms and keep on stirring till the mixture turns thick and leaves the sides of the vessel. Put the mixture in a greased thali, level the surface and sprinkle coconut nicely on top. Mark into squares. Break the squares when the vadi turns completely cold. Store in airtight containers.

Rus chi vadi

1 kilo juice of fresh, ripe mangoes. Sugar equal to the weight of the juice. 1 tsp. powdered cardamom seeds. 25 grams mixed sliced nuts. Silver foil. 1 tblsp. ghee.

Put the juice in a heavy-bottomed vessel and cook over a slow fire till it turns thick. Mix in the above ingredients and keep on stirring till it turns thick and leaves the sides of the vessel. Remove from fire and put in a greased thali. Cover with foil and set aside to turn cold. Cut into squares and store in airtight container.

Tamatar chi vadi

1 kilo tomatoes, peeled, pureed and depiped. 1

kilo sugar. 1 coconut, finely grated. 1 tsp. coarsely pounded cardamom seeds.

Fry coconut in little ghee to a pale golden colour. Mix coconut with the rest of the above ingredients and put in a heavy-bottomed vessel and cook over a slow fire till the mixture turns thick and starts leaving the sides of the vessel. Put the mixture in a greased thali level and surface and set aside to turn cold and hard. Cut into small squares and store in airtight container.

Kaju chi vadi

500 grams cashewnutss. 500 grams sugar. 1 tblsp. cardamom seeds, coarsely powdered. A few drops essence of kewda. Silver foil.

Pound cashewnuts to a fine powder. Mix together cashewnuts and sugar and put in a heavy-bottomed vessel along with cardamoms and keep on stirring over a slow fire till the mixture turns thick and leaves the sides of the vessel. Mix in the essence. Remove from fire and put in a greased thali. Cover with foil and set aside to turn cold and hard. Cut into diamond shapes and store in airtight container.

Rava chi vadi

1 cup each of rava, ghee, finely grated coconut and milk. 2 cups sugar. 1 tsp. coarsely pounded cardamom seeds. A few each of almonds, pistachios and cashewnuts. A few drops essence of saffron.

Pound all the nuts coarsely. Mix together rava,

coconut, ghee, milk and sugar and put in a heavy-bottomed vessel. Keep on stirring over a slow fire till the mixture turns thick and leaves the sides of the vessel. Mix in the essence and cardamom and remove from fire. Put in a greased thali, level the surface and sprinkle nuts on top. Set aside to turn cold and hard and then cut into any shape you like. Store in air tight container.

Narial chi vadi

2 big coconuts, finely grated. 1 kilo sugar. 500 grams khoya. 1 tsp. essence of rose. 1 tblsp. coarsely pounded cardamom seeds. 25 grams blanched and sliced almonds and pistachios. Silver foil.

Put 250 grams water in sugar and prepare a syrup of one-thread consistency. Mix in the coconut and khoya and mix till the mixture turns smooth. Add the rest of the above ingredients and keep on stirring over a low fire till the mixture turns smooth and leaves the sides of the vessel. Put the mixture in a greased thali, level the surface and cover with foil. Set aside to turn cold and hard and then cut into any shape you like. Store in airtight container.

Batate chi vadi

500 grams potatoes, boiled, peeled and mashed. 250 grams khoya. 350 grams sugar. 1 cup ghee. 25 grams each of finely sliced cashewnuts and chironji. 1 tsp. powdered cardamom seeds. A few drops essence of saffron. Silver foil.

Put 1 cup water in sugar and prepare a syrup of one-thread consistency. Remove from fire and keep it warm. Heat ghee and fry the potatoes and khoya to a light golden colour. Mix in the syrup, nuts and cardamoms and keeep on stirring till the mixture turns thick and leaves the sides of the vessel. Remove from fire and put in a greased thali. Level the surface, cover with foil and set aside to turn cold and hard. Cut into any shapes you like and store in airtight container.

Parshad cha sheera

¼ cup each of rava and sugar and ghee. 1½ cups milk. 1 small ripe banana, peeled and sliced into thin rounds. 1 tsp. cardamom powder. A few essence of saffron. A few mixed sliced nuts.

Heat ghee and fry the rava to a light red colour. Add sugar, milk and cardamoms and keed on stirring over a slow fire till the mixture turns thick. Remove from fire and mix in the bananas and essence. Garnish with nuts before serving.

Narial che rus cha sheera

¼ cup rava. ¼ cup sugar and ghee. 1½ cups coconut milk. 1 tsp. powdered cardamoms. A few fried raisins, chironji and cashewnuts. A few drops essence of saffron.

Heat ghee and fry the rava to a red colour. Pour in the coconut milk and add sugar and cook over a slow fire till the mixture turns thick.

DELIGHTS FROM MAHARASHTRA

Mix in the rest of the above ingredients and remove from fire. Serve hot.

Ambache rus cha sheera

¼ cup each of rava, sugar and ghee. 1 cup each of milk and juice of ripe sweet mango. 1 tsp. powdered cardamoms. A few fried raisins, cashewnuts and chironji.

Heat ghee and fry rava to a red colour. Mix in the sugar and milk and cook till thick. Pour in mango juice and add cardamoms and continue cooking till it turns thick. Remove from fire and serve garnished with nuts and raisins.

Batate cha sheera

250 grams potatoes, boiled, peeled and mashed. ¼ cup sugar. 1 cup milk. 2 tblsps. each of cream and ghee. 1 tsp. powdered cardamom seeds. 1 tblsp. sliced coconut. A few blanched almonds, chironji, cashewnuts and raisins.

Fry raisins, nuts and coconut to a golden colour and set aside. Heat ghee and fry the potato paste to a light brown colour. Add sugar and milk and keep on stirring over a slow fire till the mixture turns thick. Mix in the cardamoms and cream and remove from fire. Serve hot garnished with nuts, raisins and coconut.

Modakas

400 grams rice flour. A big pinch salt. ½ tsp. sugar. 1 tsp. oil.

For filling......2 coconuts, finely grated. 200 grams each of sugar and finely grated jaggery. 100 grams khoya. 1 tsp. powdered cardamom seeds. 1 tblsp. poppy seeds.

Roast poppy seeds. Mix together coconut, sugar and jaggery and cook over a slow fire till the mixture turns thick. Add khoya, cardamoms and poppy seeds and cook till dry. Remove from fire and set aside. Weigh the flour and take three-fourths of its weight of water. Boil the water and put in salt, sugar and oil. Mix and then stir in the flour gradually mixing all the time. Cook till the flour turns thick and leaves the sides of the vessel. Remove from fire, cool till bearable hot and knead to a smooth dough with oiled hands. Divide the dough and the filling into equal number of portions. Now take one portion of dough and place in the centre of your left palm. Press with the right thumb at the centre and sides with the fingers. Form into a cup and stuff with the filling. Gather the cup into seven or eight pleats and then carefully close at the top after pressing them together. Steam for about 15 minutes. Serve hot.

Cucumber cake

2 cups finely grated peeled cucumber. ½ cup sugar. 3 tblsps. finely grated coconut. ¼ tsp. turmeric powder. A big pinch each of sugar and soda bicarbonate. 50 grams chopped cashewnuts. 1½ cups semolina.

Fry the semolina to a red colour in a little ghee. Mix together cucumber, coconut, sugar, turmeric, soda, salt and then mix in the semolina. The amount of semolina will vary according to juice in the vegetable. Do not add any liquid. Stir in the cashewnuts and put in a greased baking dish. Put a few blobs of butter on top and bake in a slow oven till the cake sets and is nice brown on the top.

Dudhpak

1 litre milk. 1½ tblsps. rice. A few each of blanched almonds, pistachios, chironji, raisins and cashewnuts. 1 tsp. cardamom powder. A few drops of essence or rose or saffron. 100 grams sugar. Silver foil.

Wash and soak the rice in water for a few hours and then drain out the water. Fry the nuts and raisins and slice them. Heat a vessel and sprinkle 1 tblsp. water in it, then pour in the milk and bring to a boil, reduce heat to simmering and put in the rice and cook till it turns thick. Mix in the essence and nuts and remove from fire. Serve chilled or hot covered with foil.

Karanjia

2 cups refined flour. 2 tblsps. hot melted ghee. Dash of salt. ¼ cup flour. ½ cup finely grated dry coconut. ¼ cup poppy seeds. 4 tblsps. raisins. 1 tblsp. cardamom seeds. 1 cup ground sugar. ¼ tsp. grated jaiphal.

Mix together salt and refined flour. Rub in hot ghee then add enough water to form a stiff dough. Cover and set aside for half an hour. Heat 4 tblsps. ghee and fry flour with coconut, poppy seeds, cardamoms and raisins to a golden colour. Mix in the sugar and jaiphal and remove from fire. Divide the dough and the filling into equal number of portions. Roll out each portion of dough as thinly as you can with the help of a little dry flour. Place the filling on one-half of the round and fold over like half-moon. Seal the edges together. Deep fry one karanjia at a time to a pale golden colour. Drain, cool nicely and store in airtight container.

Shrikhand

2 cups thick curds. 4 tblsps. ground sugar. 1 tsp. rose water. A few drops essence of saffron. 1 tblsp. milk 25 grams each of blanched and sliced almonds and pistachios. 1 tblsps. charoli 1 tblsp. cardamom powder.

Put curds in a clean piece of cloth and tie loosely. Hang the bag for a couple of hours in order to enable all the liquid to drip through. Beat up the curds nicely with the help of a fork. Sprinkle cardamom powder over it and set aside for 5 minutes. Tie a strong cloth over a dekchi and take a small quantity of both sugar and curds, mix thoroughly over the cloth and put in a bowl. When all the sugar and curd has been used up, mix in essence, milk and rose water. Garnish with nuts and chill. Serve with piping hot puries.

Rote

2 cups suji or semolina. 1 cup sugar. $1\frac{1}{2}$ cups milk. $\frac{1}{2}$ cup ghee. A few drops of saffron. 1 tsp

cardamom powder. A big pinch of grated jaiphal. 25 grams each of blanched and sliced almonds, raisins and pistachios. 1 tblsp. chironji.

Mix together suji, milk, sugar and ghee thoroughly and set aside for half an hour. Then put in the rest of the ingredients, mix well and put the mixture in a greased baking dish. Sprinkle 1 tblsp. of sugar on top and bake in a moderate oven till the cake turns firm and the top turns a nice almond colour.

Anarasa

750 grams rice. 500 grams grated jaggery. 50 grams sugar. 100 grams poppy seeds. 25 grams each of almonds and pistachios. 1 tsp. cardamom powder. A few drops essence of rose.

Soak rice in water for 3 days continuously changing water daily. After 3 days, dry it indoors and grind to a fine powder. Mix in jaggery and sugar and a little melted ghee to make a dough. Do not add any water. Shape the dough into balls and keep them covered for 3 days. On the 4th day, pound each ball till soft. Pound together almonds and pistachios coarsely and mix with poppy seeds. Mix cardamom powder and essence into the pounded mixture. Form the mixture into round biscuits and press nut mixture on both the sides of each biscuit. Deep fry over a very slow fire till they turn golden coloured. Drain, cool and store in airtight tin.

Bhareli keli

6 rajeli bananas. ½ coconut, finely grated. 1 tblsp. cardamom powder. 250 grams grated jaggery, 2 cups coconut milk.

Mix together 2 tblsps. ghee, coconut and cardamoms and cook over a slow fire till thick. Peel and slice bananas halfway through on one side and fill nicely with the filling. Put them side by side in a vessel and pour coconut milk on top. Cook till all the moisture is absorbed.

Basundi

1 litre milk. 25 grams each of almonds, pistachios, cashewnuts and raisins. 1 tblsp. chironji. 1 tsp. powdered cardamoms. A few drops essence of rose. A few rose petals. 100 grams sugar.

Fry the nuts and raisins and slice finely. Boil milk till it is reduced to 1 cup only. Mix in sugar and keep on boiling till it is dissolved. Mix in the rest of the ingredients and serve chilled.

Kaju poli

250 grams each of maida and cashewnuts. 250 grams powdered sugar. ½ cup milk. 1 tsp. powdered cardamoms. A few drops essence of saffron. A big pinch salt.

Mix together salt and flour. Rub in 2 tblsps. of ghee and then add enough water to form a stiff dough. Soak the cashewnuts in water whole night. Next morning, drain out the water and grind to a fine paste. Mix together sugar, cashewnuts. milk and cardamoms and cook over a slow fire till the mixture turns thick and leaves the sides of the vessel. Mix in the essence and remove from fire. Divide the dough and the filling into equal number of portions. Shape each portion of dough into a round ball and roll out each ball into a round disc. Spread fiilling mixture nicely and evently over one round and cover with the other round. Seal the edges nicely then roll out into a bigger round or chapati with the help of a little dry flour. Shallow fry to a golden brown colour. Serve either hot or cold.

Khoya poli

500 grams maida. 250 grams khoya. 125 grams gram flour. 125 grams powdered sugar. A few drops essence of saffron. 1 tsp. powdered cardamoms. Milk.

Mix maida with a pinch of salt, then rub in 2 tblsps. melted ghee. Add saffron and enough milk to form a stiff dough. Roast khoya. Fry gram flour in little ghee to a golden colour. Add khoya, sugar and cardamoms and stir well till the mixture turns smooth. Divide the dough and the filling into equal number of portions then make polis as shown in the above recipe.

Puran poli

250 grams flour. A pinch of salt.

For filling......125 grams channa dal. 1 cup

powdered sugar. 1 tsp. powdered cardamoms. ¼ coconut, finely grated. 1 tsp. each of til and khus-khus.

Mix together salt and flour. Rub in 2 tblsps ghee and prepare a stiff dough. Fry coconut, poppy seeds and til to a red colour. Soak dal in water for a few hours, drain thoroughly and then cook with little water till tender and completely dry. Grind dal until very smooth. Add ground sugar, coconut and rest of the filling ingredients. Mix nicely. Now divide the filling and the dough into equal number of portions and form polis as shown in the recipe entitled "Kaju poli".

Coconut poli

250 grams maida. Salt to taste.

For filling......1 coconut, finely grated. 1½ cups sugar. 1 tblsp. coarsely pounded cardamoms. A few drops essence of rose or kewda.

Put salt into maida and add enough water to form a stiff dough. Cook coconut and sugar together over a low fire till the mixture turns thick and sticky. Remove from fire and mix in cardamoms and essence. Divide the filling and the dough into equal number of portions and form into polis as shown in the recipe entitled "Kaju poli".

Sweet khaja

500 grams maida. 200 grams sugar. A few drops yellow food colouring. 1 tblsp. cardamom pow-

der. 1 tsp. either essence of rose, kewda or saffron.

Cover sugar with water and set aside till it melts and turns into a syrup. Mix together the rest of the above ingredients and add the syrup to form a stiff dough. If the dough is not of desired consistency add more flour or water to make into a right consistency. Divide the dough into small balls and roll out each ball into a thin and round puri. Cut into neat diamonds and make any design you like with different colours on each peace. Deep fry till crisp and golden. Drain, cool and store in airtight container.

Besan Karanjias

500 grams refined flour or maida. 2 tblsp. rice flour.

Filling......250 grams gram flour or besan. 1 dry coconut, finely grated. 25 grams each of almonds, cashewnuts, raisins and pistachios and charoli. 2 tblsps. poppy seeds. 1 tblsp. powdered cardamoms. A big pinch grated nutmeg.

Put enough water in flour to form a stiff dough. Mix 4 tblsps. of solid ghee into rice flour and mix till fluffy. Fry the nuts, coconut, poppy seeds and raisins in ghee and slice very finely. Heat 4 tblsps. ghee and fry the gram flour to a nice golden colour. Mix in the rest of the filling ingredients and remove from fire. Now divide the dough into lime-sized balls. Roll out each ball into a thin chapati or disc. Apply a little rice paste on uppermost side of one chapati and place another chapati on top and again apply the paste. Repeat this procedure till you have assembled four chapaties. Roll the assembled chapaties lightly. Stamp out rounds and place a tblsp. of filling on one-half of the round and fold over to form half-moons. Seal and crimp the edges and deep fry over a slow fire till crisp and almond coloured. Drain, cool and store in airtight containers.

Suji Karanjia

500 grams refined, flour or maida. 75 grams suji or rava. A few drops essence of saffron. Milk. 2 tblsps. rice flour. 4 tblsps. solid ghee.

For filling......250 grams suji or rava. 250 grams powdered sugar. 25 grams each of almonds, pistachios, cashewnuts and raisins. 2 tblsps. poppy seeds. 25 grams charoli. 1 tsp. cardamom powder. A few drops of essence of saffron.

Mix together rice flour and ghee till light and fluffy. Blend together suji and flour, add saffron and a pinch of salt along with enough milk to form a stiff dough. Fry the nuts, poppy seeds and raisins to a golden colour and slice finely. Heat 5 tblsps. ghee and fry suji to a golden colour. Remove from fire and mix in the rest of the filling ingredients. Now prepare the karanjias in the same manner as shown in the above recipe.

DELIGHTS FROM MAHARASHTRA

Petha karanjia

500 grams refined flour or maida. 2 tblsp. rice flour. 4 tblsps. solid ghee. A pinch of salt.

For filling......500 grams red pumpkin, peeled and grated. 250 grams sugar, 25 grams each of almonds, cashewnuts raisins and pistachios. 1 tblsp. poppy seeds. 1 tblsp. charoli. A big pinch nutmeg. 1 tsp. cardamom powder.

Mix rice flour with ghee till light and fluffy. Mix together flour and salt along with enough water to form a stiff dough. Fry all the nuts, poppy seeds and raisins and slice them finely. Cook pumpkin without adding water till soft, mash and mix in the rest of the filling ingredients and cook till dry. Remove from fire and make the karanjias in the same manner as shown in the recipe entitled "Besan Karanjias". This is a basic recipe for making carrot, pumpkin or marrow karanjias.

Sweet chakali

6 cups rice flour. $\frac{1}{4}$ cup melted ghee. 1 cup cooked moong dal. 2 cups fine puffed rice or poha. 5 cups grated jaggery. 1 cup milk. 1 tsp. cardamom powder. A few sliced mixed nuts. A big pinch grated nutmeg.

Wash the puffed rice and squeeze dry. Dissolve jaggery in milk over a slow fire. Mix together the rest of the ingredients nicely. Add enough jaggery mixture till the mixture forms into a soft dough. Heat enough ghee for deep frying to smoking, lower the heat and press the dough through a chakali mould into the sizzling ghee. Deep fry over a slow fire till crisp and almond-coloured. Drain, cool and store in airtight tins.

Dudhdachi vadi

1 litre milk. 1 litre thick coconut milk. 100 grams blanched and ground almonds. 100 grams pounded cashewnuts. 25 grams sliced pistachios. 1 tsp. powdered cardamoms. A few rose petals. 750 grams sugar.

Put both the milks, cashewnuts, almonds and cardamoms and nutmeg over a slow fire and cook till thick, add sugar and keep on stirring till the mixture leaves the sides of the vessel. Remove from fire and put in a few drops of essence of rose. Put the mixture in a greased thali, level the surface and decorate with pistachios and rose petals. Set aside to turn cold and then cut into small pieces.

COLD DRINKS

Mango cooler

1 big raw mango. 2 full glasses of water. ½ tsp. roasted and powdered cumin seeds. A few drops essence of rose. 4 tblsps. sugar. Cracked ice.

Boil mango in water till it turns very soft. Peel, mash and then remove seed stone. Mix with the water and then strain through a fine cloth. Mix in the sugar, rose water and cumin seeds. Chill and serve with cracked ice.

Ginger cooler

Strained juice of 1 big lime. 2-inch piece ginger. 6 tblsps. sugar, 2 glasses water. Cracked ice.

Grind the ginger and extract juice. Mix with water along with lime juice and sugar. Chill and mix in cracked ice. Float sprigs of mint leaves on top before serving.

Jaggery cooler

100 grams finely grated jaggery. 2 big glasses water. Strained juice of 1 big lime. A drop of red food colouring. ½ tsp. cardamom powder. Cracked ice.

Soak jaggery whole night in water. Strain add colour, lime juice and cardamom powder. Chill and mix in ice. Serve with tiny roses floating on top.

Tamarind refresher

25 grams tamarind. Strained juice of 1 lime. 150 grams finely grated jaggery. ½ tsp. cardamom powder. A big pinch salt. 2 glasses water. Crack-

ed ice. A few drops red food colouring.

Soak tamarind in ½ glass water whole night. Soak jaggery in remaining water whole night. Strain both the jaggery and the tamarind through a cloth. Mix in the rest of the above ingredients with the exception of ice. Chill, mix in ice and float a few mogra flowers on top before serving.

Cocum Amrit

100 grams fresh, round and red cocums. Strained juice of 1 big lime. ½ tsp. cardamom powder. A few drops of essence of saffron. Sugar to taste. Cracked ice.

Mash the cocums to a fine pulp and strain out the juice through a cloth. Stir in 2 glasses of iced water along with the rest of the above ingredients. Chill, mix in ice before serving.

Mint nectar

50 grams mint. 2-inch piece ginger. A drop green food colouring. Strained juice of 2 limes. 10 tblsps. sugar. Cracked ice. 2 glasses water.

Grind and extract the juice of both mint and ginger. Strain through a cloth and mix with water along with the rest of the above ingredients with the exception of ice. Chill, mix in ice, float a few rose buds on top before serving.

PURIES & CHAPATIES

Masala puri

125 grams refined flour. ½ small bunch corriander leaves. 2 green chillies, finely sliced. 1 tsp. crushed pomogranate seeds. 4 crushed peppercorns. ¼ tsp. chilli powder. ¼ tsp. cumin seeds, pounded coarsely. Salt to suit the taste.

Mix together all the above ingredients. Rub in 1 tblsp. melted ghee and then add enough water to form quite a stiff dough. Divide the dough into lime-sized balls and roll out each ball into a little thick and round disc. Deep fry one at a time to a golden brown colour. Drain thoroughl and serve immediately with a bowl of seasoned curds.

Mithi puri

250 grams refined flour. 4 tblsps. ghee. 1 tblsp. sour curds. 2 cups sugar. Dash of salt. 1 tblsp. strained lime juice.

Blend together flour, ghee, salt and curds, then add enough water to form quite a stiff dough. Mix sugar together with 1 cup water and prepare a syrup of 1-thread consistency. Mix in lime juice and remove from fire, but keep it hot. Divide the dough into small balls and roll out each ball into round discs. Deep fry one at a time to a golden brown colour, drain thoroughly and immediately toss into the syrup. Let them steep in the syrup for 5 minutes, then drain out the puries and serve.

Sheera chapati

200 grams refined flour. 125 grams semolina. 1

tblsp. cardamom seeds pounded. 75 grams finely grated jaggery. 3 tblsps. ghee.

Form quite a stiff dough of maida with water and set aside. Heat ghee and fry the semolina to a golden colour. Add 1 cup water. When the semolina turns almost dry, put in jaggery and cardamoms and cook till the mixture turns thick and dry. Remove from fire, cool and divide into small balls. Also divide the flour into equal number of balls. Form the maida into cups, stuff with sheera. Gather the edges together and form into a smooth round cutlet, then roll into a round disc or chapati with the help of a little flour. Heat a girdle to smoking and grease it liberally with ghee. Place the chapati over it, when the undersize turns golden coloured pour a little ghee along the edges and turn over. When both the sides turn golden, remove from fire and serve hot.

Tilgul chapati

500 grams flour or rice flour. 500 grams jaggery. 50 grams gram flour. 100 grams til or sesame seeds. 50 grams peanut oil.

Clean and roast the til over dry girdle to a brown colour. Also roast gram flour to a red colour in a dry pan. Pass jaggery through a fine grater to remove all lumps. Mix together jaggery, gram flour and til and set aside. Rub oil into the flour and add enough water to form a stiff dough. Divide the dough into small balls and roll out each ball into a round disc. Spread jaggery mixture liberally over one round and cover with the other round. Seal the edges nicely, then with the help of a little dry flour roll out as thinly as you can being careful not to break the chapati. Bake on a dry girdle. Then cool and serve with pure ghee.

Other JAICO Books of Interest

Indian Cookery by E. P. Veeraswamy

Indian Cooking by Savitry Chowdhary

Curries of India by Harvey Day

Art of Vegetarian Cookery
by Betty Wason

Good Food from India
by Shanti Rangarao

Indian Cookery by E. Malhan

Regional Indian Recipes
by R. Muthachen

Simplified Indian Cookery
by R. Joseph

Adventures in Indian Cooking
by Mary Atwood

Party Recipes by Sylla Bhaisa

PARTY RECIPES

Sylla Bhaisa

ENTERTAINING CAN BE FUN...

provided you are sure that your guests have eaten well and have appreciated the food you have cooked for them.

In this unusual cookbook, Sylla Bhaisa gives over 350 recipes that takes the risk out of entertaining. Every recipe included in the book has been tried by her and the proportions have been perfected to guarantee a sumptuous meal. The simple, step-by-step instructions leave no room for error and yet variations are possible if you want the individual touch.

Next time you throw a party, keep PARTY RECIPES within reach. It is a cookbook you can rely on.

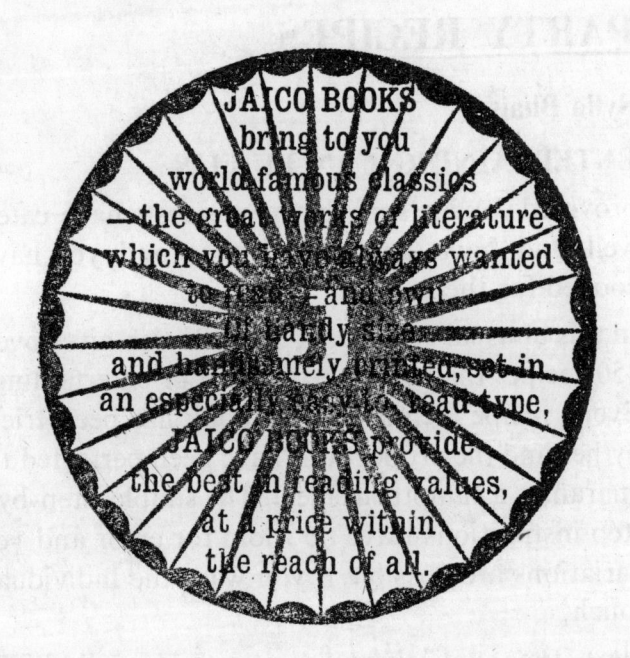

JAICO BOOKS
bring to you
world-famous classics
—the great works of literature
which you have always wanted
to read—and own.
Of handy size
and handsomely printed, set in
an especially easy-to-read type,
JAICO BOOKS provide
the best in reading values,
at a price within
the reach of all.